Human Body

Fun Activities, Experiments, Investigations, and Observations!

Grades 4-6

WITHDRAWN

This book has been correlated to state, national, and Canadian provincial standards. Visit *www.carsondellosa.com* to search for and view its correlations to your standards.

Credits

Authors: Sue Carothers and Elizabeth Henke

Production: Quack & Company, Inc.

Illustrations: Milton Hall

Cover Design: Matthew VanZomeren

Photo Credit: LifeArt image © 2001, Lippincott Williams & Wilkins. All rights reserved.

ISBN 0-88724-954-X

Table of Contents

Systems of the Human Body
Building Blocks of the Body 4
Let's Get Organized 5
Systems of the Human Body 6

The Skeletal System
KWL Chart 7
How the Skeletal System Works 8–9
A Spine-Tingling Experience 10
The Framework of the Body 11
Shoulder and Arm Bones 12
Hip and Leg Bones 13
Hands and Feet 14
Mr. Matchmaker 15
A Joint Effort 16
Let's Join In 17
No Bones about It! 18
Bone Up on This! 19

The Muscular System
KWL Chart 20
How the Muscular System Works 21–22
Masses of Muscles 23
The Muscle Mystery 24
Muscle Mania 25
Muscling Up on the Muscular System 26
Those Aching Muscles 27
Voluntary and Involuntary Muscles 28
Researching Skeletal & Muscular Systems . . .29

The Digestive System
KWL Chart 30
How the Digestive System Works 31–32
The Digestive System 33
Inside of a Tooth 34
Open Wide! 35
Chew on This! 36
Down the Hatch! 37
Go the Digestive Distance 38
Saliva Makes It Sweet 39
Where's the Beef? 40
A Journey through the Digestive System 41
Differences in Digestive Systems 42
Researching the Digestive System 43

The Respiratory System
KWL Chart 44

The Respiratory System (continued)
How the Respiratory System Works 45–46
The Respiratory System 47
Take a Deep Breath 48
Breathe On! 49
The Respiratory System 50
Full of Hot Air 51
Researching the Respiratory System 52

The Circulatory System
KWL Chart 53
How the Circulatory System Works 54–55
The Beat Goes On 56
The Blood 57
It's Heartwarming 58
Circulatory System 59
Your Beating Heart 60
Don't Miss the Boat! 61
Researching the Circulatory System 62

The Excretory System
KWL Chart 63
How the Excretory System Works 64
The Excretory System 65
Excretory Organs and Functions 66

The Endocrine System
KWL Chart 67
How the Endocrine System Works 68
The Endocrine System 69
The Gland Finale 70

The Nervous System
KWL Chart 71
How the Nervous System Works 72–73
The Body's Control Center 74
Neurons .75
Job Descriptions 76
A Brain Booster 77
The Nervous System 78–79
Researching the Nervous System 80

The Five Senses
KWL Chart 81
Skin Deep 82
The Great Cover-Up 83
Sensing Heat and Cold 84
How the Sense of Sight Works 85

Table of Contents

The Five Senses (continued)
The Eyes Have It 86
Seeing Is Believing 87
More Than Meets the Eye 88
Turn a Blind Eye 89
Sense of Sight 90
How the Sense of Hearing Works 91
Now Hear This 92
I'm All Ears 93
Hear Ye! Hear Ye! 94
Hammer It Out! 95
How the Sense of Smell Works 96
Don't Be Nosy! 97
Nosing Around 98
The Nose Knows .99
How the Sense of Taste Works 100
A Tasty Puzzle 101
You've Got Good Taste 102
Senses of Smell and Taste 103
A Map of the Tongue 104

What's That Memory I Smell? 105
Stimulating Those Senses 106

Health and Nutrition
Some Handy Tips for Hand Washing 107
Eating Healthy 108
Healthy Essentials 109
Product Information 110
Healthy Hunting .111

Body Fun
Writing a Cinquain Poem 112
Off the Top of Your Head 113
More Human Body Idioms 114
Human Body Analogies 115
I Don't Belong Here 116
A Body Makeover 117
Patterns .118–123
Answer Key 124–128

Introduction

Human Body is a useful and creative way for teachers and parents to enhance a textbook unit about the human body or present a unit if a textbook is not available.

The book includes an overview of each major body system that introduces and explains the organs and vocabulary relating to that system. To access prior knowledge and summarize concepts learned, a KWL Chart is included for each system. Following each KWL Chart is an exercise matching terms with definitions. This is a useful tool to assess what students already know *(K)* and could be given at the end of the unit to see what students have learned *(L)*. The crossword puzzles do not include Word Banks so they serve as good review tests. Also included are diagrams of each system and of individual organs with Word Banks for labeling. Magic squares, word searches, and anagrams within each unit are fun ways to familiarize students with vocabulary, improve spelling skills, and learn interesting facts. Many of these exercises can also be used for assessment purposes. The book contains connections to language arts related to the human body with such activities as guided research pages and creative writing activities.

To reinforce and strengthen students' understanding of concepts and to develop their science-process skills, a variety of activities, investigations, observations, demonstrations, and models are included. These projects require few materials, include easy-to-follow directions, and are designed to be both stimulating and enjoyable.

Name _____

Building Blocks of the Body

Human bodies are made up of trillions of tiny building blocks called cells. Most cells are too small to be seen without using a microscope. There are over 200 different kinds of cells in human bodies. Each type of cell has a different shape and size, and each type has a different job to do in the body. At any moment, there are billions of cells in the body that die and are replaced by new ones.

Cells in the body do not work alone. Cells of the same kind work together to make up tissue. A tissue is a group of cells that are alike and perform a certain job together. Just as cells are grouped into tissues, the tissues of the body are grouped together into organs. Organs, such as the brain, heart, lungs, and stomach are the main parts of the body and are arranged into systems. A system is a group of organs that work together to perform one or more jobs.

Label the cell type that is pictured and described below.

Word Bank

| muscle cell | bone cell | nerve cell |
| red blood cell | white blood cell | epithelial cell |

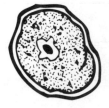

1. _____

forms tissue that makes bones

2. _____

forms tissue that can stretch

3. _____

forms tissue that covers and protects

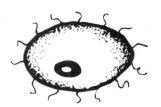

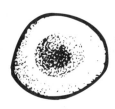

4. _____

kills germs that attack the body

5. _____

carries oxygen and food to cells and takes away the carbon

6. _____

carries messages to and from the brain

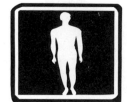

Name _____

Let's Get Organized

Each system of the body is made up of organs that work together to perform a specific function. Each organ does a certain job as part of the system. Some organs belong to more than one system.

Write the name of each organ under the name of the system to which it belongs. Not all lines will be used.

brain	bones	thyroid gland	stomach	kidney
muscles	spinal cord	lungs	pituitary gland	ureter
liver	bladder	joints	trachea	heart
diaphragm	esophagus	small intestine	blood vessels	ligaments
urethra	nerves	adrenal glands	tendons	pancreas

Skeletal System	Muscular System	Digestive System	Nervous System
_____	_____	_____	_____
_____	_____	_____	_____
_____	_____	_____	_____
_____	_____	_____	_____
_____	_____	_____	_____

Circulatory System	Respiratory System	Endocrine System	Excretory System
_____	_____	_____	_____
_____	_____	_____	_____
_____	_____	_____	_____
_____	_____	_____	_____
_____	_____	_____	_____

Name _____

Systems of the Human Body

The body is made up of an amazing group of systems. The systems of the body all work together and need each other to keep the body healthy and well. Each system has certain functions. The systems of the body are made up of groups of organs that work together to carry out the functions of that system.

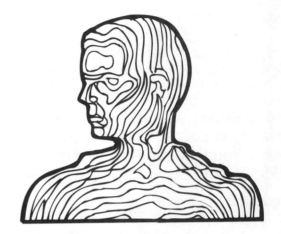

Write the name of the body system that matches the description of the functions.

Word Bank

| muscular | excretory | respiratory | circulatory |
| digestive | endocrine | nervous | skeletal |

---

1. _____ The functions of this system are to support and move the body and protect some of the organs.

2. _____ The function of this system is to control all movement in the body.

3. _____ The function of this system is to change food into a form that can be used by the body.

4. _____ The function of this system is to bring in oxygen for the body to use and to take away carbon dioxide.

5. _____ The function of this system is to excrete, or remove, wastes from the body.

6. _____ This system helps to control the body by releasing chemicals called hormones.

7. _____ The function of this system is to carry materials such as food and oxygen to the cells throughout the body.

8. _____ The functions of this system are to receive and carry messages to control the body and all of its parts.

Name _____

KWL Chart
The Skeletal System

The main functions of the skeletal system are to support the body, allow the body to move, protect organs, store minerals, and produce blood cells.

Before you begin learning about the skeletal system, complete the first two sections of the chart below. Under **K**, list what you already know about the system. Under **W**, list what you would like to find out about the system. After you have studied the system, go back to the chart and list what you learned under **L**.

K What I know	W What I want to find out	L What I learned

Name _____

How the Skeletal System Works

To find out what you already know about the skeletal system, write a word or words from the Word Bank to complete each definition.

Word Bank

flat	long	short	bones	skeletal system
joints	fixed	gliding	calcium	calcification
hinge	pivot	marrow	ligaments	ball-and-socket
irregular	cartilage	fracture	moveable	partially moveable

_____ 1. The ____ has several functions. It supports the body, permits movement, protects internal organs, stores minerals, and produces blood cells.

_____ 2. The human skeleton of an adult is made up of a total of 206 ____ , which give the basic shape to the body and make up a framework to which muscles are attached. At birth, humans have over 300 bones, but some of them fuse together.

_____ 3. Besides bones, the skeleton also contains connective tissue called ____ , which is flexible and tough. This type of rubbery tissue is present in the tip of the nose, the outer ear, and wherever two bones meet.

_____ 4. The places in the skeleton where two or more bones meet are called ____ , and these can be grouped into three basic types.

_____ 5. One type of joint that allows no movement at all is called a ____ joint. Examples of this type of joint are found in the hip and in the skull.

_____ 6. Another type of joint that allows a small amount of movement is called a ____ joint. The spinal column contains this type of joint.

_____ 7. A ____ joint, like those found in the knees and shoulders, allows full movement of bones.

_____ 8. The bones in a joint are cushioned by cartilage, which keeps them from rubbing together. They are held together by strong bands of connective tissue called ____ .

_____ 9. ____ bones are the chunky, wide bones of the feet and wrists.

Name _____

_____ 10. Another type of moveable joint is called a _____ joint. It allows movement in only one direction, like on a door. Knees, elbows, and the first and second bends in fingers are examples of these types of joints.

_____ 11. A _____ joint, a moveable joint that allows movement in many directions, is formed where the rounded end of one bone fits into the socket of another bone. The hips and the shoulders contain this type of joint.

_____ 12. The last type of moveable joint is called a _____ joint because it allows rotating movement from side to side, like in the first and second neck vertebrae. In this type of joint, one bone twists within the cup or ring of another.

_____ 13. Bones include about 30% living tissue, including bone cells, blood, blood vessels, nerves, and fat. The center of a bone has a space, or cavity, containing a soft tissue called ____ in which new blood cells are produced.

_____ 14. Bones are covered by a tough outer membrane. Underneath this membrane is a layer of bone cells surrounded by deposits of minerals, which make the bone hard and strong. _____ is a mineral that comes from milk and milk products and is important in building strong bones.

_____ 15. Before birth, the skeleton is made mostly of cartilage. During the early years of life, the bones begin to harden as they become coated with layers of minerals. This process is called _____ .

_____ 16. There are four basic shapes of bones. Some are _____ bones, like in our legs and arms.

_____ 17. Some bones have a _____ shape. These include plate-like bones such as the ribs and shoulder blades.

_____ 18. There are several types of moveable joints in the body. One type is called a _____ joint because it allows smooth, sliding movements. Examples of this type of moveable joint are the wrist and ankle.

_____ 19. Some bones, such as the vertebrae, have very odd shapes and do not fit into any other category. These are called _____ -shaped bones.

_____ 20. A break in a bone is called a _____ .

Name _____

A Spine-Tingling Experience

The spinal column, or backbone, provides the main upright support for the body. It is made up of 27 small ring-like bones in a series, called vertebrae. The vertebrae enclose and protect the spinal cord, which is made of delicate nerve tissue. There are discs of cartilage between each of the vertebrae that act as cushions, or shock absorbers, in the spinal column. The vertebrae are not all exactly alike, even though they look similar. Some vertebrae are attached to the ribs, and some in the pelvic region are joined together.

Label each region of the vertebral column in the diagram of a backbone.

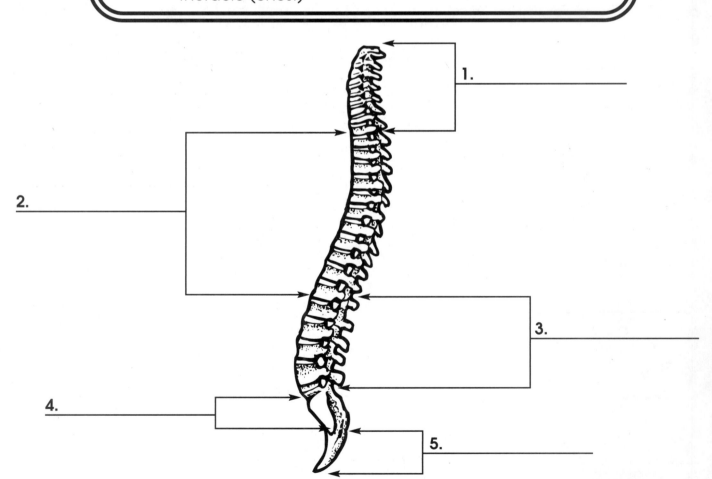

Word Bank

Scientific Name (Common Name)

cervical (neck)   lumbar (lower back)

coccygeal (tailbone)   sacral (pelvic girdle)

thoracic (chest)

1. _____

2. _____

3. _____

4. _____

5. _____

Name _____

The Framework of the Body

Label the major bones of the body in the diagram of the skeletal system.

Word Bank
Scientific Name (Common Name)

cranium (skull)
carpals (wrist bones)
pelvis (hipbone)
tarsals (ankle bones)
tibia (shinbone)
phalanges (fingers and toes)

clavicle (collarbone)
patella (kneecap)
scapula (shoulder blade)
fibula (lower leg bone)
rib cage (ribs)

radius (lower arm bone)
vertebrae (backbone)
femur (thighbone)
ulna (lower arm bone)
mandible (jawbone)
humerus (upper arm bone)

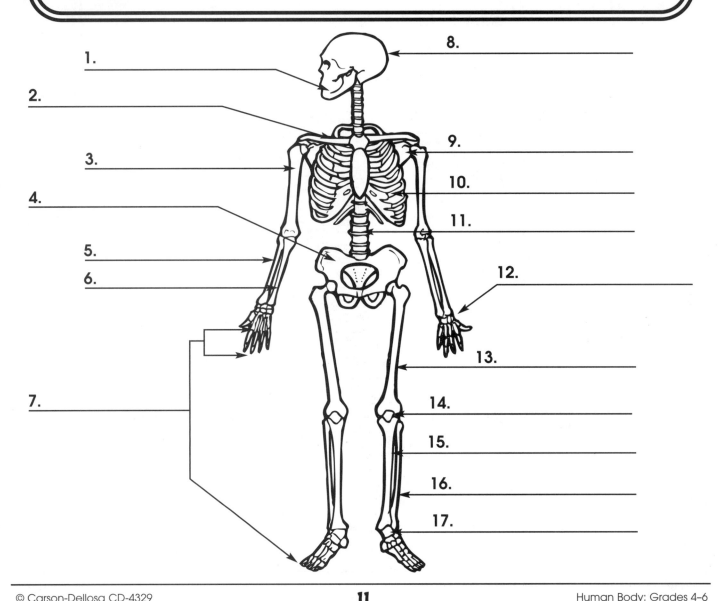

1. _____

2. _____

3. _____

4. _____

5. _____

6. _____

7. _____

8. _____

9. _____

10. _____

11. _____

12. _____

13. _____

14. _____

15. _____

16. _____

17. _____

Name _____

Shoulder and Arm Bones

Use the words from the Word Bank to label the diagram of the shoulder and arm.

Word Bank
Scientific Name (Common Name)

scapula (shoulder blade)   clavicle (collarbone)

humerus (upper arm bone)   ulna (lower arm bone)

radius (lower arm bone)

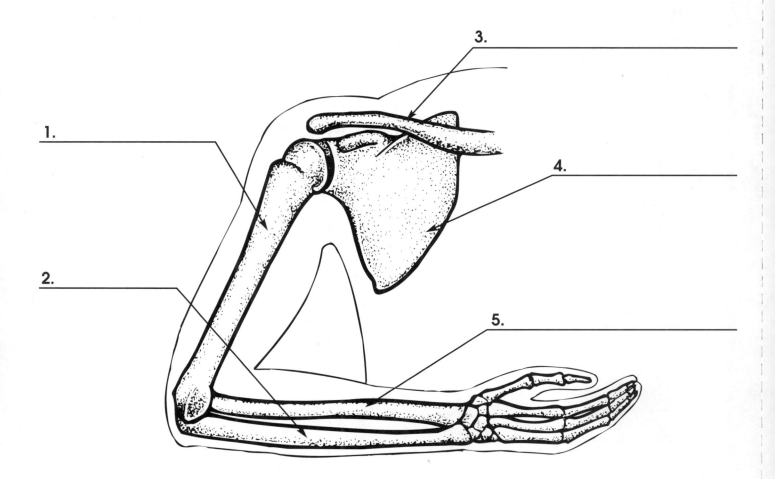

3.

1.

4.

2.

5.

Name _____

Hip and Leg Bones

Use the words from the Word Bank to label the diagram of the hip and legs.

Word Bank
Scientific Name (Common Name)

femur (thighbone)   patella (kneecap)   pelvis (hipbone)

fibula (lower leg bone)   tibia (shinbone)   coccyx (tailbone)

lumbar vertebra (lower back vertebra)

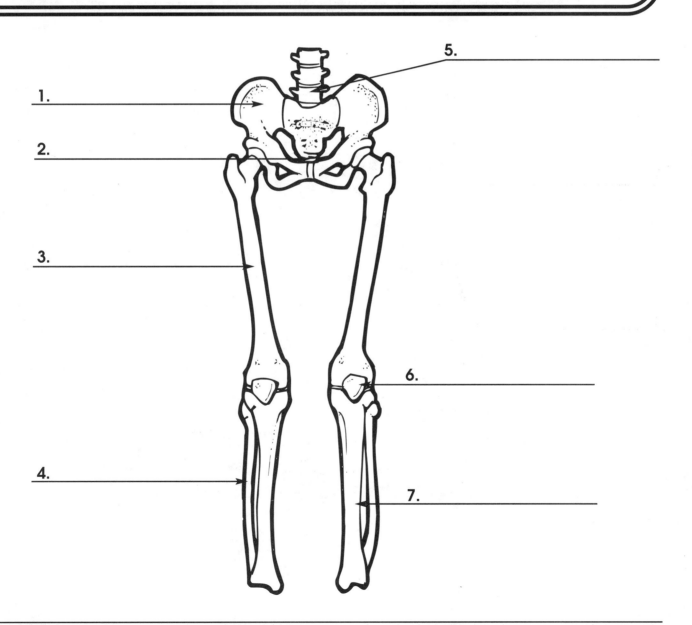

1. _____

2. _____

3. _____

4. _____

5. _____

6. _____

7. _____

Name _____

Hands and Feet

Use the words from the Word Bank to label the bones of the hand and foot.

Word Bank
Scientific Name (Common Name)

phalanges (finger bones)	carpal (wrist)	phalanges (toe bones)
metatarsals (foot bones)	tarsal (ankle)	metacarpal (palm)

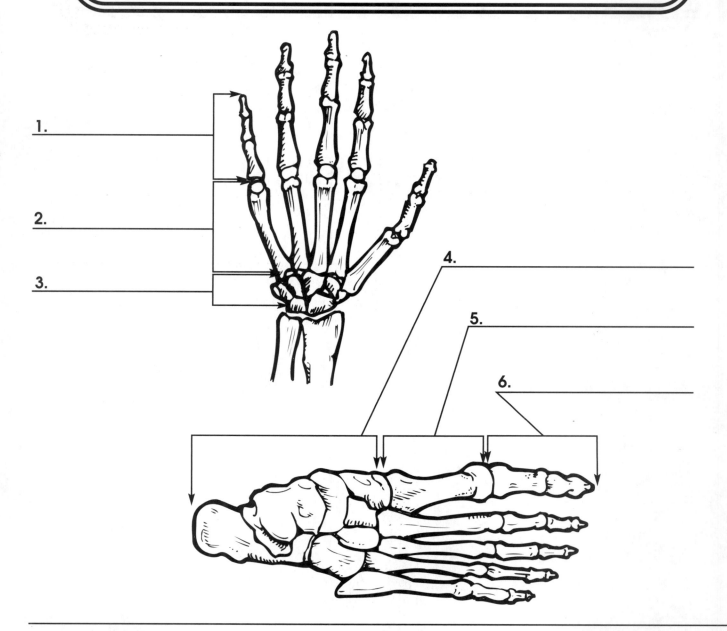

1. _____

2. _____

3. _____

4. _____

5. _____

6. _____

Name _____

Mr. Matchmaker

Most bones have a scientific name and a common name.

Write the words from the Word Bank in the spaces to match the common name of each bone to its scientific name.

> **Word Bank**
> **Common Name**
>
> arm bone   thighbone   kneecap   skull   foot bones
> finger bones   hipbone   backbone   ribs   jawbone

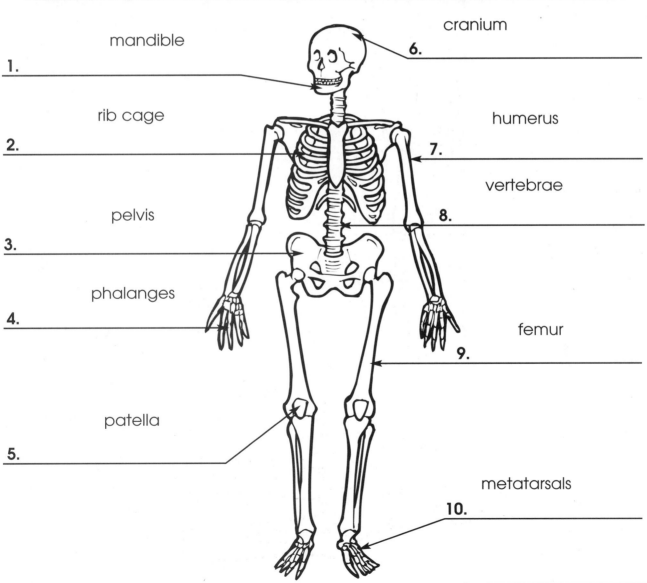

cranium

mandible

1. _____

6. _____

rib cage

humerus

2. _____

7. _____

vertebrae

pelvis

8. _____

3. _____

phalanges

4. _____

femur

9. _____

patella

5. _____

metatarsals

10. _____

Name _____

A Joint Effort

A joint is where two or more bones are joined together. There are many different kinds of joints in the body.

Write the name of each type of joint in the spaces below.

   A. Fixed joints, as found in the skull, do not move.

   B. Partially moveable joints, as found between the vertebrae of the back, allow some movement of bones.

   C. Moveable joints allow full movement of bones.

      1. Ball-and-socket joints, which are found in the shoulder, allow the bones to swing in almost any direction.

      2. Hinge joints, such as the joints in the elbow and knee, allow movement in one direction.

      3. Pivot joints, which are found in the neck, form when one bone rests and rotates from a certain point.

      4. Gliding joints, such as the wrist, are formed when two bones that can move separately meet.

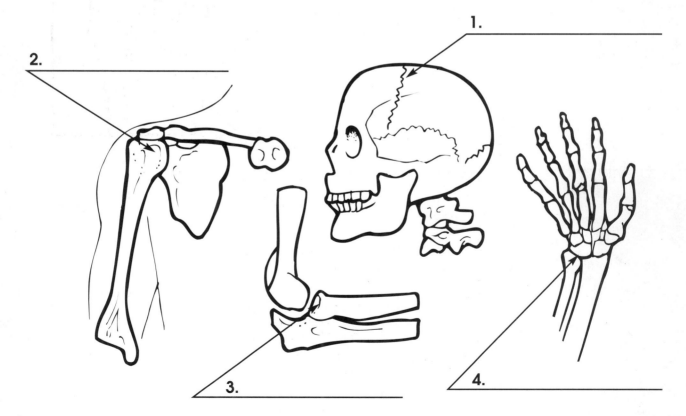

1. _____

2. _____

3. _____

4. _____

Name _____

Let's Join In

Classify the following joints by writing the letter naming the type of joint in the blank before each joint. For moveable joints, write the letter and the correct number.

A. Fixed joints allow no movement of bones.

B. Partially moveable joints allow some movement of bones.

C. Moveable joints allow full movement of bones.

    1. Ball-and-socket joints allow movement in any direction.

    2. Hinge joints allow movement in only one direction.

    3. Pivot joints allow rotating movement from side to side.

    4. Gliding joints allow sliding movement back and forth.

_____ 1. knee

_____ 2. elbow

_____ 3. vertebrae

_____ 4. skull

_____ 5. wrist

_____ 6. neck

_____ 7. shoulder

_____ 8. hip

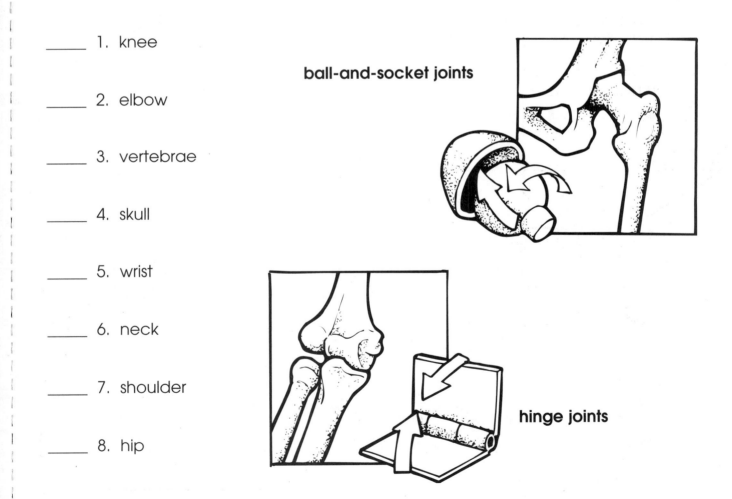

ball-and-socket joints

hinge joints

Name _____

No Bones about It!

Circle the words from the Word Bank in the puzzle. The words can be found horizontally, vertically, and diagonally.

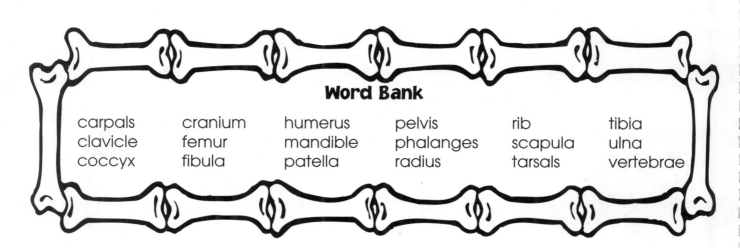

Word Bank

carpals	cranium	humerus	pelvis	rib	tibia
clavicle	femur	mandible	phalanges	scapula	ulna
coccyx	fibula	patella	radius	tarsals	vertebrae

o	c	c	x	y	c	a	r	p	o	f	r	a	d	i
f	s	e	g	n	a	l	a	h	p	i	e	b	t	y
i	d	s	e	v	x	y	z	b	a	b	v	m	h	s
t	i	b	r	s	e	e	i	f	l	u	e	a	u	z
a	p	a	m	b	c	r	c	i	l	l	r	n	m	r
r	d	e	u	f	g	a	t	b	e	a	t	d	e	a
s	h	i	l	l	g	k	p	e	l	x	e	i	r	d
a	l	m	n	v	n	o	p	u	b	i	b	b	u	i
l	x	x	a	t	i	a	r	s	l	r	r	l	s	u
s	a	y	r	v	w	s	s	c	x	a	a	e	t	s
d	b	z	c	a	r	p	a	l	s	f	t	e	a	r
e	c	e	l	c	i	v	a	l	c	e	y	c	r	i
a	i	b	i	t	o	u	l	l	h	m	x	b	s	d
m	a	n	b	i	l	c	e	p	a	t	e	l	l	a

Human Body: Grades 4–6

Name _____

Bone Up on This!
Calcium in Bones

Calcium is a very hard mineral that helps make bones and teeth strong. Calcium comes from the foods we eat. To have healthy bones and teeth, it is important to eat foods such as milk, yogurt, cheese, and leafy, green vegetables.

 Question:
What is the purpose of calcium in bones?

Materials Needed:

- 2 cleaned chicken leg bones
- white vinegar
- 2 jars with lids

Procedure:

A. Put a cleaned chicken leg bone in a jar filled with vinegar and put the lid on the jar. (Vinegar will dissolve the calcium from the bone.)

B. Put the other bone into an empty jar and put the lid on the jar.

C. Wait at least one week and then remove the bones from the jars. Compare them by trying to bend each bone.

Results:

How is the bone that still has calcium different from the bone that lost its calcium when it was soaked in the vinegar?

_____

Conclusions:

Why is it important to have calcium in our bones? What does calcium do for our bones?

_____

_____

_____

Describe some problems that people could have if they do not get enough calcium in their diets.

_____

_____

_____

_____

Name _____

KWL Chart
The Muscular System

The main functions of the muscular system are to produce movement of body parts and to help in digestion and circulation.

Before you begin learning about the muscular system, complete the first two sections of the chart below. Under **K**, list what you already know about the system. Under **W**, list what you would like to find out about the system. After you have studied the system, go back to the chart and list what you learned under **L**.

K What I know	W What I want to find out	L What I learned

Name _____

How the Muscular System Works

To find out what you already know about the muscular system, write a word or words from the Word Bank to complete each definition.

Word Bank

voluntary muscles	tendons	smooth muscle	cramp
involuntary muscles	strain	muscle cells	extensor
muscular system	flexor	cardiac muscle	
muscle tissue	exercise	skeletal muscle	

_____ 1. The main purpose of the _____ is to cause movement of the body parts. This system also helps with digestion and circulation. It is made up of over 600 different muscles.

_____ 2. Muscles can be divided into two main groups. The _____ are muscles that can be controlled consciously. They move when you think about what you want them to do. For example, muscles in the arms and legs can be controlled when walking or running.

_____ 3. _____ are muscles, such as the heart, that automatically do their jobs without you needing to think about it. These muscles run all the important jobs inside the body, such as breathing and digesting.

_____ 4. Every muscle in the body is made up of a particular kind of _____ .

_____ 5. There are three main kinds of muscle tissue. Muscle tissue that is attached to and moves the skeleton is called _____ . This type of muscle tissue has stripes and is a voluntary muscle.

_____ 6. _____ is the type of muscle tissue found in the walls of many organs and blood vessels in the body. It is a type of involuntary muscle tissue and does not have stripes.

Name _____

_____ 7. The type of muscle tissue that is found only in the heart is an involuntary muscle tissue called _____ . It is made of a network of striped muscle cells that never stop working.

_____ 8. The only cells in the body that can shorten (contract) are _____ . When a cell contracts, it gets shorter. When it relaxes, it returns to its original size. This contracting and relaxing of muscle cells is what makes the body move.

_____ 9. Most muscles work in pairs to produce movement. One muscle pulls a bone one way, and another pulls the bone in the opposite way. The bones are connected to the skeletal muscles with tough bands of connective tissue called ____ .

_____ 10. A ____ is a muscle that causes a joint to bend when it contracts.

_____ 11. An ____ is a muscle that causes a joint to straighten when it contracts.

_____ 12. When muscle cells ____ , or do work, they need more food and oxygen. Blood carries food and oxygen to the muscle cells, so the heart has to pump blood faster. When done regularly, this can make the muscle get bigger and more efficient.

_____ 13. A ____ is an injury caused when a muscle is overstretched.

_____ 14. A ____ is when a muscle contracts involuntarily. This can be painful and is sometimes caused by too much exercise or by not "warming up" the muscles before exercising.

Name _____

Masses of Muscles

The three types of muscle tissues found in the body are smooth, cardiac, and skeletal. Cardiac muscle is a type of involuntary muscle made up of a network of striped cells and is found only in the heart. Smooth muscle is a type of involuntary muscle made of short, non-striped cells that line the digestive tract and blood vessels. Smooth muscles have smooth, slow contractions, and they can stay contracted for long periods of time. Skeletal muscles are the muscles that move the bones of the body. They are voluntary muscles made up of bundles of long, striped cells.

Label each diagram of muscle cells. Next to each diagram, name a part of the body where this type of muscle can be found.

Type of muscle		**Where this muscle type can be found in the body**
1. _____		_____
2. _____		_____
3. _____		_____

The Muscle Mystery

To produce movement in the body, most muscles work in pairs and use teamwork. One set of muscles causes movement in one direction, and the other set of muscles causes movement in the opposite direction. As muscles contract, or become shorter, they pull the bones in a certain direction. The opposing set of muscles contracts to pull the bones in the opposite direction. The bicep and tricep of the upper arm are a good example of a muscle team at work.

Complete the explanation of movement of the upper arm.

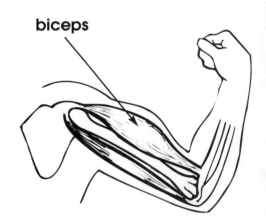

biceps

1. When the bicep _____ ,
   the arm raises.

2. As the arm raises, the tricep

   _____ .

3. When the _____ relaxes,
   the arm straightens.

4. As the arm straightens, the
   _____ contracts.

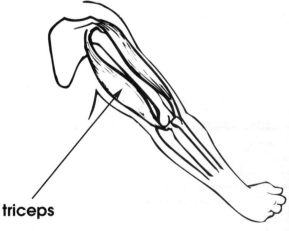

triceps

Word Bank

contracts   relaxes   biceps   triceps

© Carson-Dellosa CD-4329   **24**   Human Body: Grades 4–6

Name _____

Muscle Mania

Circle the words from the Word Bank in the puzzle. The words can be found horizontally, vertically, and diagonally.

m	i	f	l	e	x	o	n	u	s	c	l	e	e	x	t	e	s
u	e	n	l	x	t	e	s	i	o	r	m	s	s	c	l	r	k
s	x	t	v	e	w	t	i	x	a	s	t	v	u	e	x	f	e
c	t	e	s	o	s	e	r	s	r	r	n	o	q	x	r	l	l
l	e	c	w	y	l	n	a	b	a	q	v	l	u	t	s	e	e
e	x	s	a	w	s	u	o	i	d	e	i	u	i	e	t	x	t
t	p	m	a	r	c	r	n	d	k	f	g	n	j	n	m	m	a
i	x	o	y	z	d	e	a	t	n	k	h	t	k	s	n	u	l
s	t	o	x	m	p	i	h	l	a	e	d	a	m	o	o	s	m
s	e	t	e	n	d	o	a	p	u	r	t	r	u	r	p	c	u
u	n	h	s	t	r	a	i	c	n	c	y	y	s	c	a	l	s
e	d	m	f	l	e	x	e	r	m	l	s	m	c	r	r	e	c
l	m	u	s	c	l	l	e	r	p	u	h	u	u	a	d	c	l
u	u	s	v	o	l	u	n	t	r	a	s	s	m	s	a	e	e
s	s	c	a	r	p	m	h	i	g	k	a	c	d	p	c	l	z
m	f	l	e	x	o	r	j	i	h	y	b	l	l	s	x	l	b
c	x	e	x	e	r	c	i	s	e	x	c	e	o	e	y	s	e

Word Bank

strain	involuntary muscle	smooth muscle
cramp	muscle cells	cardiac muscle
exercise	muscle tissue	voluntary muscle
tendons	muscular system	extensor
flexor	skeletal muscle	

Name _____

Muscling Up on the Muscular System

Complete the crossword puzzle.

Across

3. a muscle, such as the heart muscle, that does its job without thinking about it
10. a muscle that causes a joint to straighten when it contracts
11. a type of muscle tissue found in the walls of organs and blood vessels
12. an injury caused by a muscle being overstretched

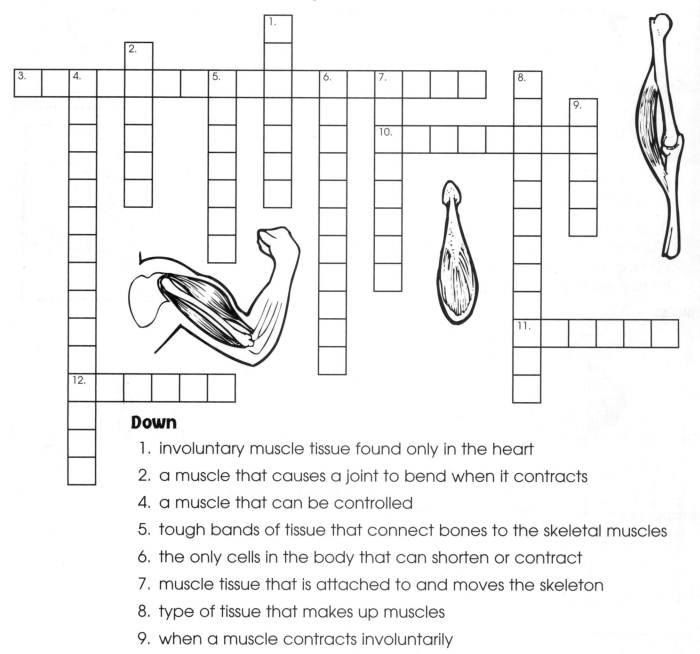

Down

1. involuntary muscle tissue found only in the heart
2. a muscle that causes a joint to bend when it contracts
4. a muscle that can be controlled
5. tough bands of tissue that connect bones to the skeletal muscles
6. the only cells in the body that can shorten or contract
7. muscle tissue that is attached to and moves the skeleton
8. type of tissue that makes up muscles
9. when a muscle contracts involuntarily

Human Body: Grades 4-6

Name _____

Those Aching Muscles

When we exercise or do work, our muscles get tired. This is because of a buildup of waste products in the muscles. Our muscle cells can contract many times in a second. When muscles contract, they use food and oxygen. The more muscles are used, the faster they need to be supplied with more fuel and oxygen, so the heartbeat rate and breathing rate increases. Producing extra energy without oxygen causes a chemical waste product called lactic acid to accumulate in the muscle cells. This buildup of lactic acid makes our muscles slow down and become exhausted.

 Question:
How much take work does it take for a muscle to become fatigued?

Materials Needed:
- string
- small weight or rock
- stopwatch or clock with a second hand

Procedure:

A. Cut a piece of string about 15 inches long.

B. Tie a weight or a small rock to one end of the string.

C. With a partner, count the number of times you can lift the weight with your finger in a two-minute time period.

D. Wait two minutes and repeat step C for a total of five trials with two-minute rest periods between each trial.

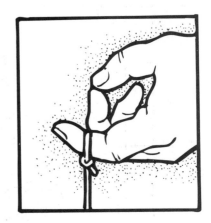

Results:

Trial	Number of finger lifts in 2 minutes
1	
2	
3	
4	
5	

Conclusions:

Could you do more, fewer, or the same number of finger lifts each trial?

_____

What is your explanation for what you observed in this experiment?

_____

_____

Name _____

Voluntary and Involuntary Muscles

Some of the movements in the body are controlled by voluntary muscles. These are muscles that respond when we consciously move them. Other movements happen without our thinking about them. These movements are controlled by involuntary muscles. Some muscles can be both voluntary and involuntary. You will see examples of all three types in the following activity.

Question:
What is the difference between voluntary and involuntary muscles?

Materials Needed: mirror

Procedure:
A. Move your arm up and down. Lift up one of your feet and put it back down.
B. Use the mirror to look at your eyes and observe the size of your pupils (black spots in the middle of your eyes). Shade one eye with your hand for a moment, then remove it and observe the size of the pupil in each eye.
C. Put your hand over your heart and feel its beat.
D. Use the mirror again and observe your eye for 30 seconds. Count the number of times that you blink.
E. Count the number of breaths that you take in 15 seconds.

Results:
1. Did your arms and feet move because you decided to move them? _____
2. Did your arms and feet ever move besides when you decided to move them? _____
3. Did the size of your pupil change after you covered your eye? _____
4. Can you change the size of your pupil without changing the amount of light? _____
5. Can you slow down or speed up your heartbeat while sitting? _____
6. Can you make your heart beat only when you want it to? _____
7. How many times did your eyes blink in 30 seconds? _____
8. Do your eyes blink without you deciding to blink? _____
9. Can you blink your eyes faster or more slowly? _____
10. How many times did you breathe in 15 seconds? _____
11. Do you breathe without thinking about it? _____
12. Can you speed up or slow down your breathing rate? _____

Conclusions:
Classify the muscles listed as **voluntary, involuntary,** or **both**.
1. arm muscles _____
2. heart _____
3. muscles that cause you to blink _____
4. muscles that cause you to breathe _____
5. leg muscles _____
6. muscles that control your pupil _____

28

Name _____

Researching the
Skeletal and Muscular Systems

Below is a list of common diseases or illnesses of the skeletal and muscular systems. Choose one from the list to research. Use the information you find to answer the following questions.

arthritis	muscular dystrophy
scoliosis	osteoporosis
cerebral palsy	Lou Gehrig's disease

Which disorder did you choose? _____

What is the cause of this disorder? _____

_____

_____

_____

_____

How does this disorder affect the body? What are the symptoms?

_____

_____

_____

_____

What is the treatment for this disorder? _____

_____

_____

_____

_____

What other interesting facts did you learn? _____

_____

_____

_____

References: _____

_____

Name _____

KWL Chart
The Digestive System

The main function of the digestive system is to break down food and prepare it to be absorbed by the blood.

Before you begin learning about the digestive system, complete the first two sections of the chart below. Under **K**, list what you already know about the system. Under **W**, list what you would like to find out about the system. After you have studied the system, go back to the chart and list what you learned under **L**.

K What I know	W What I want to find out	L What I learned

30

Name _____

How the Digestive System Works

To find out what you already know about the digestive system, write a word or words from the Word Bank to complete each definition.

Word Bank

gastric juice	digestion	large intestine	rectum	tongue
appendix	enzymes	intestinal juice	saliva	villi
peristalsis	esophagus	mechanical	small intestine	bile
chemical	salivary glands	gallbladder	pancreas	stomach

_____ 1. ____ is the process by which food is broken down into substances that can be used by the cells of the body.

_____ 2. In the digestive system, food undergoes two kinds of digestion. ____ digestion occurs as the food is broken into smaller pieces.

_____ 3. Mechanical digestion prepares the food for ____ diges-tion, which is the process by which foods are chemically changed into simpler substances.

_____ 4. Digestion begins as soon as food enters the mouth, where the teeth and tongue work together to physically break down the food into smaller pieces. As chewing takes place, a secretion from the ____ softens and lubri-cates the food.

_____ 5. This secretion from the salivary glands is called ____ .

_____ 6. Saliva contains ____ , substances that speed up chemical reactions and break down large starch molecules into smaller molecules of sugar.

_____ 7. The ____ helps push food to the back of the mouth where it is swallowed.

_____ 8. After being swallowed, the food passes into a muscular tube called the ____ , which connects the mouth to the stomach.

_____ 9. Food in the esophagus is squeezed toward the stomach by contraction and relaxation of the muscles in the esophagus. This muscular action, known as ____ , also helps to move food through the rest of the digestive tract.

Name _____

_____ 10. Food takes about six seconds to travel from the mouth to the ____ , a j-shaped sac that stores and further digests the food.

_____ , _____ 11. Food remains in this organ for about four to six hours as it is mixed with digestive liquids such as ____ , a mixture of enzymes and acids that chemically break down protein. Food is broken into smaller pieces through a churning action of three layers of muscles in the stomach wall, which is lined and protected from the strong digestive juices by a layer of mucus.

_____ 12. A ring of muscle at the end of the stomach controls the flow of food by opening and closing every few minutes to allow the liquid food to flow into the ____ , a very long, coiled, tube-like organ.

_____ 13. The final steps of digestion occur in the small intestine. One type of digestive liquid that is added here is called ____ , which is produced in the liver and breaks down fats in foods.

_____ 14. A storage sac called the ____ holds the bile that is produced in the liver.

_____ 15. Pancreatic juice is another digestive juice added in the small intestine. It is produced in the ____ .

_____ 16. ____ , which is made in the walls of the small intestine, works together with the pancreatic juice to chemically break down the food.

_____ 17. The nutrients from the digested food are then absorbed into the bloodstream through tiny finger-like structures called ____ that line the inner wall of the small intestine. Nutrients from the digested food are carried by the blood from the villi to the cells of the body.

_____ 18. Materials that are not digested move into the ____ , which is a wider but shorter tube than the small intestine.

_____ 19. There is a little pouch called the ____ located where the small intestine joins the large intestine. It has no known purpose in our bodies, but it can sometimes become infected and have to be removed.

_____ 20. At this point in the process, no more digestion occurs. Water and salts are taken out of the waste material in the large intestine. The remaining solid wastes, called feces, are the end product of digestion and are stored in the ____ .

Name _____

The Digestive System

Use the words from the Word Bank to label the diagram of the digestive system.

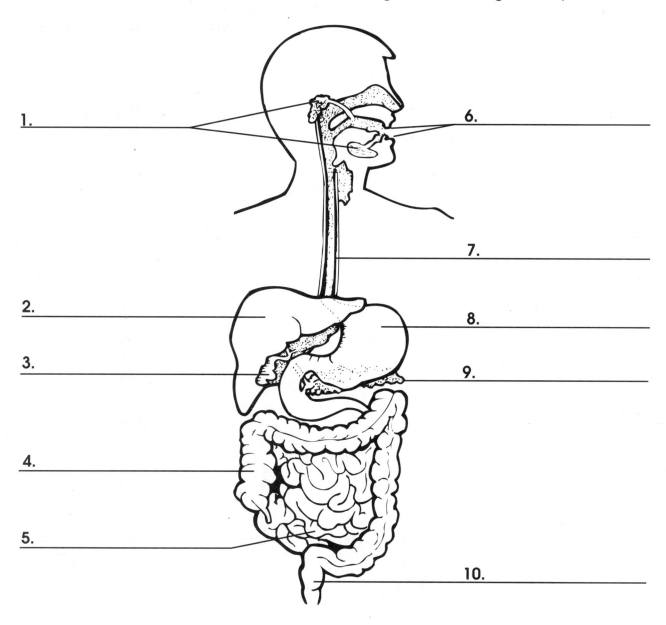

1. _____

2. _____

3. _____

4. _____

5. _____

6. _____

7. _____

8. _____

9. _____

10. _____

Word Bank			
salivary glands	stomach	gallbladder	mouth
pancreas	liver	rectum	large intestine
small intestine	esophagus		

Name _____

Inside of a Tooth

Teeth contain the hardest substance in the body. The inner part of the tooth, called the pulp, has blood vessels and nerves. It is the living part of the tooth. The next layer, called dentin, is like bone, but harder. The outer coating of the tooth is made mostly of minerals and is called enamel. Cementum is the outer coating of the tooth's root that holds it in place.

Label the diagram showing the parts of a tooth.

Word Bank

dentin	enamel	crown	bone
gums	pulp	root	cementum

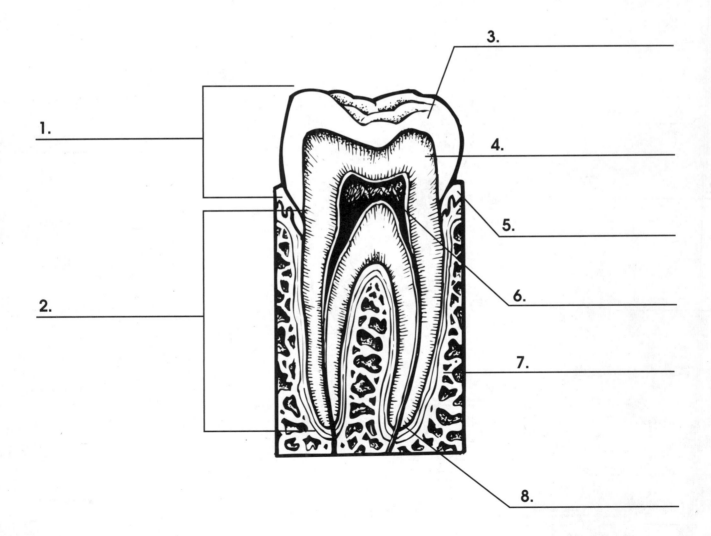

1. _____

2. _____

3. _____

4. _____

5. _____

6. _____

7. _____

8. _____

Name _____

Open Wide!

There are four different kinds of teeth. Each type of tooth is specialized for breaking apart food in a certain way. The front teeth are for biting. They are large and flat and are called incisors. Next to the incisors are the canine teeth. These teeth have a sharp point and are used for tearing the food. The premolars are next to the canine teeth and are used to grind and mash the food. The molars are the flat teeth in the back of the mouth which are also used for grinding.

Use the words from the Word Bank to label the diagram with the four types of teeth. Words will be used more than once.

Word Bank

molars   incisors   premolars   canines

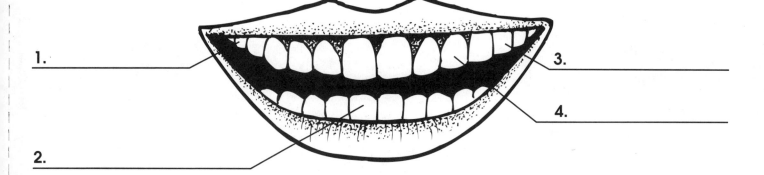

1. _____

2. _____

3. _____

4. _____

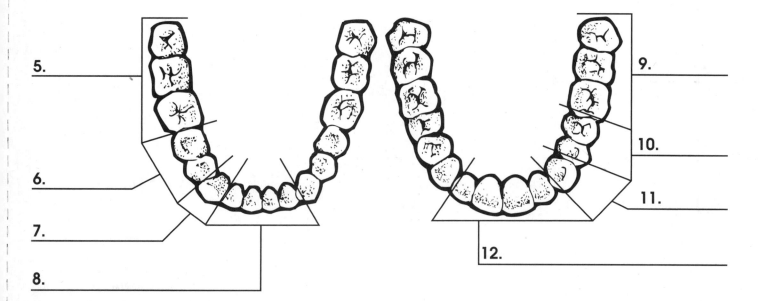

5. _____

6. _____

7. _____

8. _____

9. _____

10. _____

11. _____

12. _____

35

Name _____

Chew on This!

Match each word or words in List I with its description from List II. Write the number in the box of the matching letter. To discover the magic number, add a row, column, or diagonal. The answer should always be the same!

List I

____ A. salivary glands

____ B. esophagus

____ C. appendix

____ D. mouth

____ E. small intestine

____ F. large intestine

____ G. rectum

____ H. anus

____ I. stomach

____ J. gallbladder

____ K. pancreas

____ L. liver

____ M. villi

____ N. bile

____ O. peristalsis

____ P. digestion

List II

2. finger-like structures that cover the inner wall of the small intestine

3. a large, lobed organ that produces bile

4. a small pouch, located on an end of the large intestine, which serves no purpose

5. a short, wide tube in which water is absorbed from undigested food

6. a gland that produces pancreatic juice

7. a liquid produced by the liver that helps digest fats

8. a long, coiled tube in which food is digested and absorbed

9. the opening through which food passes into the body

10. a muscular tube which connects the throat to the stomach

11. stores solid wastes until they leave the body

12. process by which the body changes food so it can be used to supply energy

13. a J-shaped, muscular sac that stores food and helps to digest it

15. opening through which feces leave the body

16. glands that produce saliva

17. organ where bile is stored

18. squeezing motion that pushes food through the digestive system

A	B	C	D
E	F	G	H
I	J	K	L
M	n	O	P

Magic number

_____

Name _____

Down the Hatch!

Circle the words from the Word Bank in the puzzle. The words can be found horizontally, vertically, or diagonally.

```
s  g  b  l  a  r  g  e  i  n  t  e  s  t  i  n  e
t  a  i  a  o  s  j  y  p  d  p  m  u  h  o  e  n
o  l  l  b  r  t  g  l  a  w  u  t  t  i  p  p  i
m  l  i  i  e  o  b  x  n  t  d  u  t  o  a  m  t
a  b  v  t  v  m  i  d  c  y  o  s  w  n  i  o  s
h  l  d  e  i  a  l  e  i  m  e  w  c  e  x  u  e
c  a  i  m  l  c  r  u  k  g  a  r  e  u  m  h  t
a  d  g  e  l  h  e  y  i  d  e  a  n  u  s  t  n
p  d  e  b  a  d  d  e  g  a  h  s  v  i  l  l  i
p  e  s  a  p  k  g  f  s  l  p  d  t  l  r  r  l
e  r  r  e  v  i  l  i  u  e  a  a  v  i  e  e  l
n  u  t  a  p  p  e  n  d  i  x  n  n  l  o  c  a
s  u  g  a  h  p  o  s  e  d  r  s  d  c  t  n  m
x  a  n  u  j  p  e  r  i  s  t  a  l  s  i  s  s
```

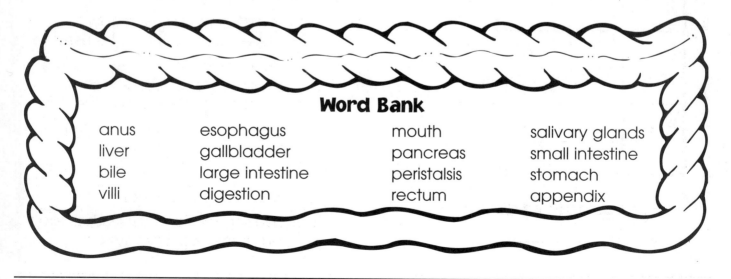

Word Bank

anus	esophagus	mouth	salivary glands
liver	gallbladder	pancreas	small intestine
bile	large intestine	peristalsis	stomach
villi	digestion	rectum	appendix

Human Body: Grades 4–6

Name _____

Go the Digestive Distance

From the time food enters the mouth until wastes are expelled, food has traveled a distance of more than nine meters (30 feet) through the digestive tract.

Unscramble the parts of the digestive system to see how far food travels through each organ. Construct a bar graph comparing the distances.

Part of Digestive System

1. humot __ __ __ __ __

2. aeghopssu

__ __ __ __ __ __ __ __ __

3. tsomhca

__ __ __ __ __ __ __

4. aslml eistinten

__ __ __ __ __

__ __ __ __ __ __ __ __ __

5. erlga eeiinntts __ __ __ __ __

__ __ __ __ __ __ __ __ __

Average Length

7.5 centimeters (3 inches)

25 centimeters (10 inches)

25 centimeters (10 inches)

550–670 centimeters (18–22 feet)

92-184 centimeters (3-6 feet)

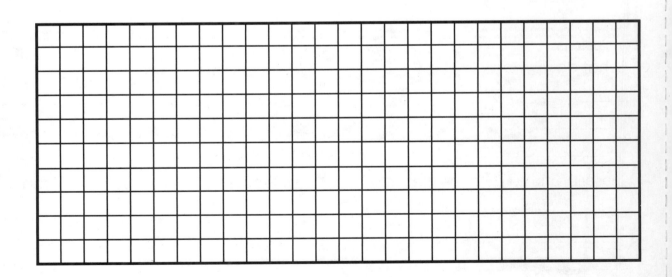

Part of Digestive System

Average Length (centimeters)

Name _____

Saliva Makes It Sweet
Digestion of Starch

The first steps in digestion take place in the mouth as the teeth cut, tear, and grind the food while the tongue mashes the food against the roof of the mouth. Saliva is squirted into the food to moisten and soften it. The mouth makes close to 500 milliliters (1/2 quart) of saliva each day. Saliva contains chemicals called enzymes, which break down the starches in the food. The enzyme in saliva that breaks down starch into sugar is called amylase.

? **Question:**
How does saliva help digest food? **?**

Materials Needed:
• unsalted soda crackers

Procedure:
A. Take several bites of an unsalted soda cracker and chew thoroughly, but DO NOT swallow the cracker. Keep the chewed cracker in your mouth for about five minutes.
B. As the cracker remains in your mouth, see if you can detect any change in its taste.

Results:
Did you detect any change in the taste of the cracker? _____ If so, describe.

_____

_____

Conclusions:
What do you think the saliva does to the starch in the cracker?

_____

_____

_____

Describe some of the ways that saliva helps to digest food.

_____

_____

_____

_____

Name _____

Where's the Beef?

Digestion of Protein

Before the body can use food, it must be broken down and absorbed into the bloodstream from the small intestine. Proteins, which are found in foods such as meat and eggs, are broken down by enzymes in the small intestine. There are about 700 different enzymes in the body. One enzyme that helps digest protein, called papain, is found in meat tenderizer.

? **Question:**
How do enzymes help us digest protein? **?**

Materials Needed:
- 2–4 teaspoons of lunch meat or ground beef
- 1 teaspoon of meat tenderizer
- 2 small jars with lids
- water

Procedure:

A. Put 1–2 teaspoons of lunch meat or ground beef in a small jar. Add water to the jar to cover the meat. Put the lid on the jar and label this jar "water."

B. Put 1–2 teaspoons of the same kind of meat in the other jar. Cover the meat with the same amount of water that you put in the first jar. Then, add one teaspoon of meat tenderizer. Put the lid on the jar and label this jar "protein."

C. Let both jars stand for two days. Then, observe the meat in the jars.

Results:

Did you detect any differences between the meat in the two jars? _____
If so, describe.

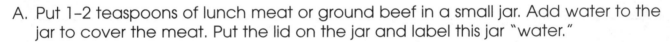

_____

Conclusions:

How do you think papain helps in the digestion of proteins?

_____

_____

_____

_____

Name _____

A Journey through the Digestive System

Choose one of your favorite foods and write a story about the journey your food takes through the entire digestive system. Be sure to describe what happens at each step of the digestive process.

_____

_____

_____

_____

_____

_____

_____

_____

_____

_____

_____

_____

_____

_____

_____

_____

_____

Name _____

Differences in Digestive Systems

Research to find out about digestion in different kinds of animals, such as rodents (mice, squirrels, etc.) or ruminating animals (cows, deer, etc.). Compare the way these animals digest food to the way humans digest food. Do all animals digest food in the same way? Is digestion in animals the same as it is in humans?

_____

_____

_____

_____

_____

_____

_____

_____

_____

_____

_____

_____

_____

_____

_____

_____

_____

_____

Name _____

Researching the Digestive System

Below is a list of common diseases or illnesses of the digestive system. Choose one from the list to research. Use the information you find to answer the following questions.

appendicitis	diabetes	hepatitis
colitis	gallstones	pancreatitis
colorrectal cancer	heartburn	ulcers

Which disorder did you choose? _____

What is the cause of this disorder? _____

_____

_____

How does this disorder affect the body? What are the symptoms?

_____

_____

_____

_____

What is the treatment for this disorder? _____

_____

_____

_____

_____

What other interesting facts did you learn? _____

_____

_____

_____

_____

References: _____

_____

_____

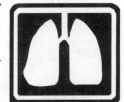

Name _____

KWL Chart
The Respiratory System

The main function of the respiratory system is to bring oxygen into the body and take away carbon dioxide.

Before you begin learning about the respiratory system, complete the first two sections of the chart below. Under **K**, list what you already know about the system. Under **W**, list what you would like to find out about the system. After you have studied the system, go back to the chart and list what you learned under **L**.

K What I know	W What I want to find out	L What I learned

44

Name _____

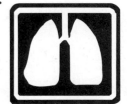

How the Respiratory System Works

To find out what you already know about the respiratory system, write a word or words from the Word Bank to complete each definition.

Word Bank

diaphragm	carbon dioxide	respiratory system	bronchi
epiglottis	vocal cords	capillaries	inhale
oxygen	exhale	larynx	nose
alveoli	trachea	pharynx	

_____ 1. The parts of the body that are used for breathing make up the ____ . This system provides oxygen to each of the cells of the body. Oxygen is needed by all cells to get energy from food. A waste product called carbon dioxide, given off by cells, is carried away by this system.

_____ 2. Air is inhaled through the ____ , where it is filtered, warmed, and moistened.

_____ 3. From the nose, air then passes through the ____ , which is the area behind the nose that leads to the throat.

_____ 4. The ____ , or voice box, is located at the bottom of the pharynx.

_____ 5. ____ , which produce the sounds of voices, are contained in the larynx.

_____ 6. The ____ is a flap of tissue at the top of the larynx. It prevents food from entering the windpipe by covering the larynx when food is swallowed.

_____ 7. At the bottom of the larynx is the windpipe, also known as the ____ .

_____ 8. The trachea is divided into two bronchial tubes, called ____ , which carry air to each lung.

       Human Body: Grades 4–6

Name _____

_____ 9. In each of the two lungs, the bronchi divide into smaller branches which contain millions of tiny air sacs called ____ .

_____ 10. Each alveolus is lined with tiny blood vessels called ____ .

_____ 11. ____ from the fresh air that is inhaled is added to the blood in the capillaries of the alveoli. This oxygen-rich blood is then carried to the heart, where it is pumped out to all the cells of the body.

_____ 12. The waste product ____ is given off in the gas exchange between air and blood in the alveoli. The carbon dioxide is released with the air that is exhaled, or breathed out.

_____ 13. The ____ is a dome-shaped muscle found under the rib cage which assists during inhalation and exhalation.

_____ 14. When the diaphragm contracts, it flattens. This action forces chest muscles to pull the ribs upward and outward, making the chest cavity expand, and the lungs ____ air.

_____ 15. When the diaphragm relaxes, it moves upward. This causes the ribs to move inward and downward and makes the chest cavity smaller. Air is forced out of the lungs as you ____ .

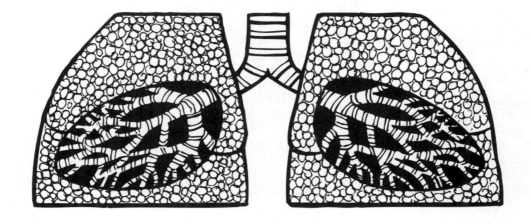

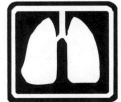

Name _____

The Respiratory System

Use the words from the Word Bank to label the diagram of the respiratory system.

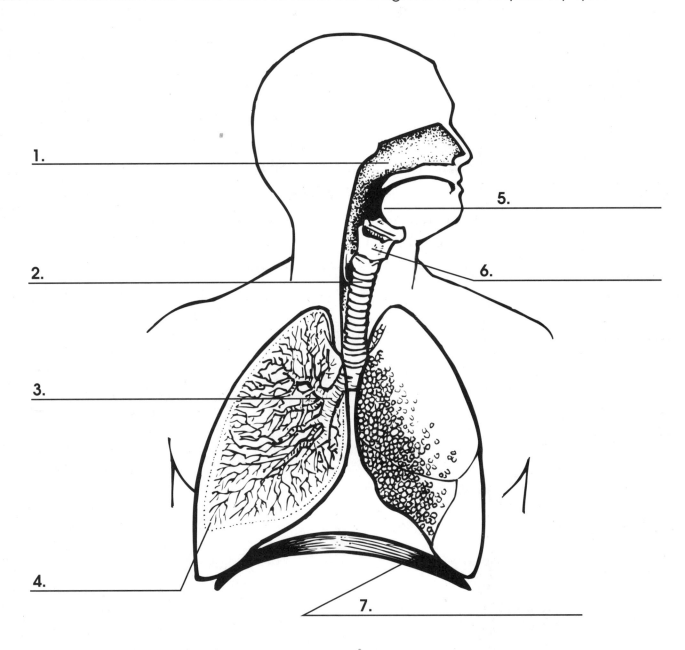

1. _____

2. _____

3. _____

4. _____

5. _____

6. _____

7. _____

Word Bank

pharynx	diaphragm	larynx
bronchial tube	epiglottis	trachea
lung		

Human Body: Grades 4–6

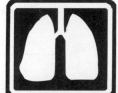

Name _____

Take a Deep Breath

Movement of air in and out of the lungs is mainly due to the contracting and relaxing of a large, involuntary muscle called the diaphragm on the floor of the chest cavity. When the diaphragm contracts, the area of the chest cavity enlarges, causing air to rush into the lungs to fill the space. This is called inhaling. When the diaphragm relaxes, the chest cavity shrinks and air is pushed back out of the lungs. This is called exhaling. The average person inhales and exhales almost 20,000 times every day.

Use the words from the Word Bank to label the parts of the respiratory system. Then, label each diagram as "inhale" or "exhale." Some words will be used more than once.

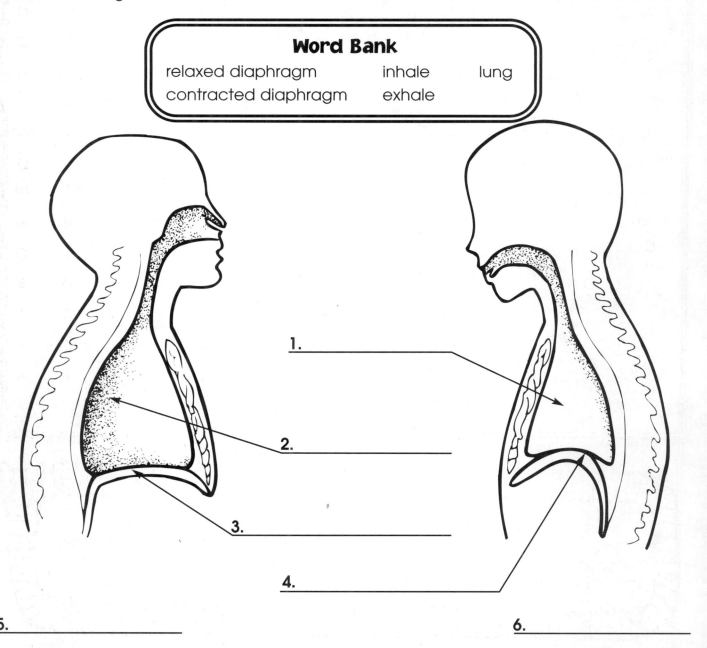

Word Bank

relaxed diaphragm	inhale	lung
contracted diaphragm	exhale	

1. _____

2. _____

3. _____

4. _____

5. _____

6. _____

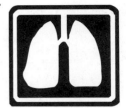

Name _____

Breathe On!

Circle the words from the Word Bank in the puzzle. The words can be found horizontally, vertically, or diagonally.

r	c	a	p	i	l	l	a	r	i	e	s	t	x	g
e	e	b	u	t	l	a	i	h	c	n	o	r	b	d
s	e	d	o	e	h	t	a	e	r	b	e	a	l	i
p	p	r	i	o	x	g	e	n	p	x	i	u	g	a
i	i	o	x	x	p	i	p	e	h	d	n	n	c	p
r	g	n	g	w	o	h	a	i	c	g	h	p	a	h
a	l	v	e	o	l	i	a	k	n	o	s	e	p	r
t	o	e	y	l	a	m	d	r	e	h	e	a	i	r
o	t	t	n	u	a	p	h	n	o	x	a	l	l	g
r	t	r	o	n	e	r	f	x	o	y	h	l	l	m
y	i	a	x	y	h	i	y	g	k	b	n	a	e	w
s	s	c	n	q	p	g	o	n	m	a	r	x	l	g
y	r	h	y	b	e	r	x	p	x	e	u	a	p	e
s	e	e	r	n	w	l	n	p	i	e	x	y	c	l
t	r	a	a	h	e	p	d	i	o	x	x	i	d	t
e	x	h	h	l	l	e	e	p	i	p	d	n	i	w
m	l	u	p	s	d	r	o	c	l	a	c	o	v	s

Word Bank

respiratory system	alveoli	exhale	pharynx	oxygen	vocal cords
carbon dioxide	nose	inhale	breathe	windpipe	epiglottis
bronchial tube	lung	larynx	trachea	capillaries	diaphragm

   Human Body: Grades 4–6

Name _____

The Respiratory System

Complete the crossword puzzle.

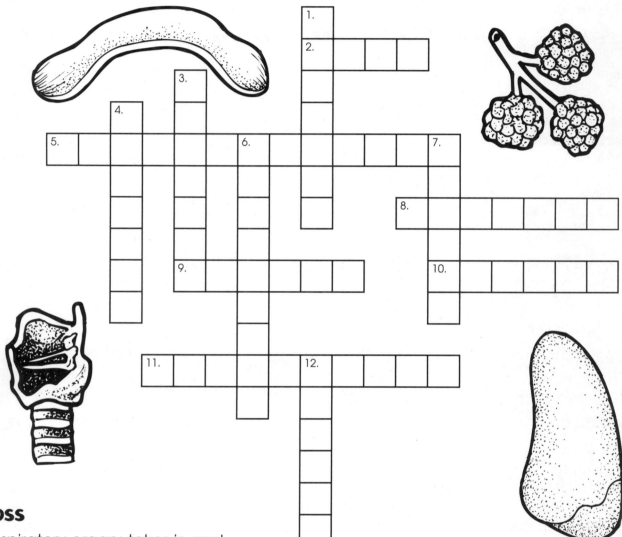

Across

2. respiratory organ; takes in and releases air

5. waste product given off in the gas exchange between air and blood in the alveoli

8. region behind the nose leading to the throat

9. to breathe in

10. voice box; contains the vocal cords

11. prevents food from entering the trachea

Down

1. group of tiny air sacs

3. the two branches of the trachea

4. a tube that carries air from the larynx to the lungs

6. sheet of muscle located between the chest and abdomen

7. to breathe out

12. colorless, odorless, tasteless gas that we breathe in

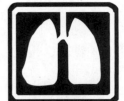

Name _____

Full of Hot Air
Lung Capacity

Each time you inhale, or breathe in, your lungs fill with air. Oxygen from the fresh air goes into the blood in the alveoli, or tiny air sacs, in your lungs. Carbon dioxide is given off and is exhaled from the lungs.

   Question:
How much air can your lungs hold?

Materials Needed:
- gallon jug
- water
- rubber or plastic tubing, 18–24 inches long
- plastic straw
- graduated cylinder or measuring cup
- dishpan or large bucket

Procedure:

A. Fill the gallon jug to the top with water.

B. Fill the dishpan or bucket with water, about one-fourth full.

C. With one hand, cover the mouth of the jug as you lower it upside down into the bucket or pan of water, allowing as little air as possible to enter the jug.

D. Place one end of the rubber tubing into the mouth of the jug.

E. Place the plastic straw in the other end of the rubber tubing and hold it there.

F. Take a deep breath and put your mouth on the straw. Blow into it until you have exhaled all the air from your lungs.

G. Slide your hand over the mouth of the jug and turn it right side up without letting any water escape.

H. Measure the amount of air that you exhaled by using the measuring cup or graduated cylinder to see how much water is needed to fill the jug back up with water. The amount of air you exhaled is the amount of water needed to fill the jug. (Note: You can measure and mark off the jug ahead of time with tape. Start at the bottom when measuring.)

Results:

My lung capacity is _____ (mL or cups).

Conclusions:

What are some factors that might affect lung capacity? Do nonsmokers have a larger lung capacity than smokers? How does the lung capacity of girls compare to that of boys? How do children's lung capacities compare to those of adults?

_____

_____

_____

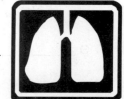

Name _____

Researching the Respiratory System

Below is a list of common diseases or illnesses of the respiratory system. Choose one from the list to research. Use the information you find to answer the following questions.

lung cancer	asthma	common cold
pneumonia	hay fever	cystic fibrosis
emphysema	bronchitis	tuberculosis

Which disorder did you choose? _____

What is the cause of this disorder? _____

_____

_____

_____

How does this disorder affect the body? What are the symptoms? _____

_____

_____

_____

_____

_____

What is the treatment for this disorder? _____

_____

_____

_____

What other interesting facts did you learn? _____

_____

_____

_____

_____

_____

References: _____

_____

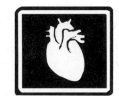

Name _____

KWL Chart
The Circulatory System

The main function of the circulatory system is to transport, or carry, materials all through the body.

Before you begin learning about the circulatory system, complete the first two sections of the chart below. Under **K**, list what you already know about the system. Under **W**, list what you would like to find out about the system. After you have studied the system, go back to the chart and list what you learned under **L**.

K What I know	W What I want to find out	L What I learned

Name: _____

How the Circulatory System Works

To find out what you already know about the circulatory system, write a word or words from the Word Bank to complete each definition.

Word Bank

oxygen	capillaries	blood	ventricle	atrium
aorta	valve	vena cava	platelets	heart
plasma	white blood cells	red blood cells	artery	veins
	circulatory system	blood vessels		

_____ 1. The purpose of the ____ is to transport materials through the body.

_____ 2. The word *circulation* comes from the word *circle*. The pathway of ____ is circular, flowing from the heart to other organs and back to the heart.

_____ 3. The ____ is the organ that pumps blood throughout the body. Blood carries oxygen and nutrients to cells and carries waste away from the cells.

_____ 4. Blood is made up of several types of cells that are in a liquid called ____ , which is mostly water and makes up more than half of the blood.

_____ 5. The cells in the blood that carry oxygen are called ____ . On average, people have about 20–25 trillion of these cells in their bodies. The body produces about three million new ones every second to replace those that die.

_____ 6. Another type of cell in the body helps the body to fight disease. These are called ____ . They are larger than red blood cells, and they capture bacteria and release chemicals that fight infections.

_____ 7. When a blood vessel is injured, there are tiny ____ in the blood that help the blood to clot and seal the cut in the blood vessel.

_____ 8. The blood travels through the body in tubes called ____ .

_____ 9. An ____ is a blood vessel that carries blood away from the heart. These blood vessels have thick muscular walls, and they divide into smaller and smaller branches which carry the blood to the body's organs.

Name _____

_____ 10. The smallest vessels are called ____ .
These blood vessels are so small that
the blood cells move through them in single file.

_____ 11. From the capillaries, the blood flows into ____ ,
which are blood vessels that carry blood back to the
heart. These blood vessels have much thinner walls
than the arteries.

_____ 12. The heart is the hardest working muscle in the body.
It contains four chambers which are connected to
each other by a ____ , or flaps of tissue that keep the
blood from flowing in the wrong direction.

_____ 13. Each of the two upper chambers of the heart is
called an ____ . These chambers collect the blood
from the veins and pump it to the lower chambers of
the heart.

_____ 14. Each of the two lower chambers of the heart is
called a ____ . The lower chamber on the left side
has a thicker wall than the one on the right because
it pumps blood throughout the body. The lower
chamber on the right pumps the blood to the lungs.

_____ 15. The ____ are the blood vessels that carry the blood
from the body to the heart into the right atrium. One
carries blood from the parts of the body above the
heart, and the other carries blood from the parts of
the body below the heart.

_____ 16. The right atrium of the heart pumps the blood
through a valve into the right ventricle. It is then
pumped into a large artery that takes the blood
to the lungs to pick up ____ and release carbon
dioxide.

_____ 17. The oxygen-rich blood flows through the veins to the
left atrium. The left atrium pumps the blood through a
valve into the left ventricle, where it is pumped
through a valve into the body's largest artery called
the ____ . From here, the blood moves to all the
organs except the lungs.

Name _____

The Beat Goes On

The heart is designed like two pumps that work side by side. The right side of the heart pumps the blood to the lungs where it takes in oxygen. The left side of the heart pumps the oxygen-rich blood out to all parts of the body.

Label the diagram of the heart.

Word Bank

right ventricle	right atrium	pulmonary veins
pulmonary artery	left ventricle	valve (use more than once)
vena cava	aorta	left atrium

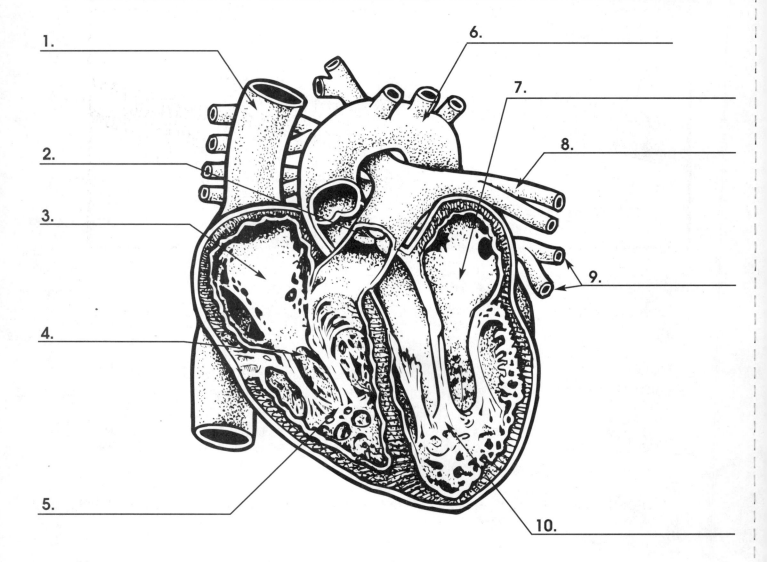

1. _____

2. _____

3. _____

4. _____

5. _____

6. _____

7. _____

8. _____

9. _____

10. _____

Name _____

The Blood

Blood travels through tubes called blood vessels as it is pumped by the heart to all parts of the body. Blood is made up of plasma, red blood cells, white blood cells, and platelets. Plasma is the liquid part of the blood. Plasma is made mostly of water. Red blood cells are disc-shaped and carry oxygen to all parts of the body. White blood cells attack germs and fight diseases. Platelets are needed for blood to clot. The clotting of blood is the process that seals cuts in blood vessels.

The sentences below tell how blood clots after a blood vessel is cut. The sentences are not in order. Use the diagram to help you number the sentences in the correct order.

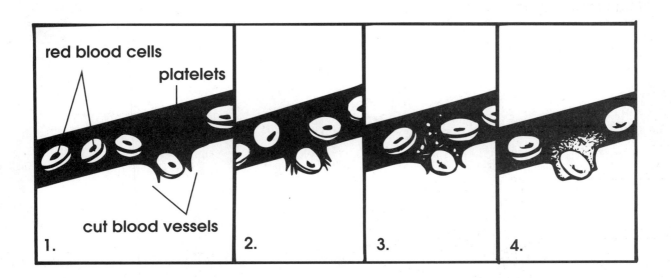

_____ The cut is filled when fibers trap platelets and some red blood cells.

_____ A blood vessel is cut, allowing blood to leak out and causing platelets to stick to the cut edges.

_____ The cut is plugged by a solid mass of platelets, fibers, and red blood cells.

_____ Platelets give off chemicals that cause proteins in the plasma to form fibers.

Name _____

It's Heartwarming

Circle the words from the Word Bank in the puzzle. The words can be found horizontally, vertically, and diagonally.

```
a  r  t  b  l  o  o  d  v  e  s  s  e  l  s  c
n  x  y  r  e  t  r  a  c  a  v  c  e  l  y  i
x  e  r  o  x  y  g  o  n  v  e  r  l  o  s  r
c  p  g  e  i  a  a  r  t  l  a  e  o  t  t  c
a  l  l  y  d  e  p  t  r  o  c  o  r  f  t  u
p  a  p  a  x  b  h  a  e  d  l  a  c  v  e  l
i  s  a  r  t  o  l  d  o  b  e  r  v  a  m  a
l  m  t  t  v  e  a  o  l  h  g  t  e  l  y  t
l  m  r  r  e  d  l  o  o  o  d  m  n  v  o  o
a  a  i  e  n  b  p  e  b  d  k  a  n  e  p  r
r  w  u  y  e  l  p  l  t  m  c  s  a  s  t  y
i  h  m  t  a  o  r  p  a  s  v  e  i  n  s  s
e  i  i  x  c  o  t  q  r  s  b  a  l  e  h  y
s  h  a  t  a  d  v  w  z  a  m  p  i  l  g  s
w  e  e  l  c  i  r  t  n  e  v  a  h  e  s  t
a  o  t  r  a  v  e  n  t  r  c  l  e  h  g  e
h  e  a  r  v  e  n  a  c  a  v  a  x  y  m  m
```

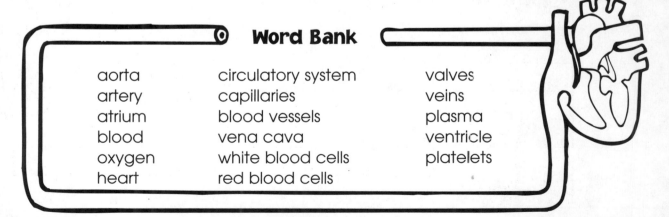

Word Bank

aorta	circulatory system	valves
artery	capillaries	veins
atrium	blood vessels	plasma
blood	vena cava	ventricle
oxygen	white blood cells	platelets
heart	red blood cells	

Name _____

Circulatory System

Complete the crossword puzzle.

Across

1. flaps of tissue that allow blood to flow in only one direction

3. red fluid that circulates throughout the body

5. blood cells that carry oxygen

7. system that transports materials throughout the body

11. a blood vessel that carries blood from the body to the heart into the right atrium

12. a blood vessel that carries blood away from the heart

13. each of the two lower chambers of the heart

14. blood cells that help the body fight disease

Down

2. an upper chamber of the heart

3. tubes that blood travels through

4. the liquid part of the blood

6. a blood vessel that carries blood toward the heart

7. blood vessels whose walls are only one cell thick

8. the largest artery of the body

9. cell fragments that help the blood to clot

10. pumps blood throughout the body

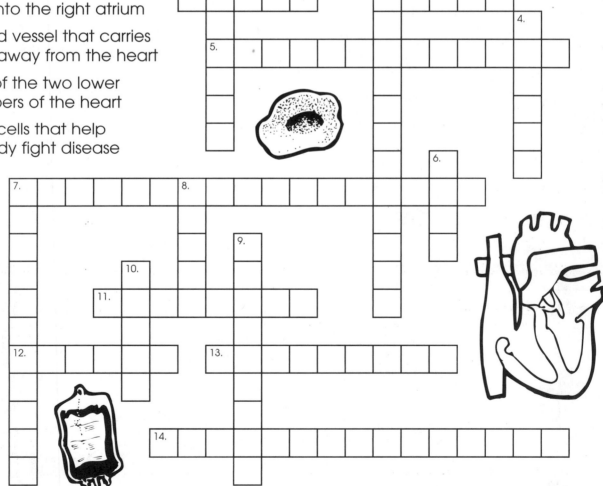

Name _____

Your Beating Heart
What Are Some Factors That Affect Your Pulse Rate?

The heart is a muscle that pumps blood through tubes, or blood vessels, inside the body. Every time your heart beats, your arteries swell a small amount as the blood pushes through. This is called your pulse. You can feel your pulse in your wrist or in the side of your neck by lightly holding your forefinger and middle finger on one of these spots.

?   **Question:**   **?**
Will exercise have an effect on your pulse rate?

Materials Needed:
• clock or watch with a second hand

Procedures:

A. Sit quietly for a few minutes. Predict and write down how many times you think your heart will beat in one minute.

B. Find your pulse in your wrist or neck. Count the number of times you can feel your pulse in one minute. Write this down. (Or, for a faster method, count how many times you can feel your pulse in 30 seconds. Multiply this number by two to find out how many times your heart beats in one minute.)

C. Run in place or climb stairs for one minute, then sit down. Immediately count and record your pulse as you did in step B.

D. Continue sitting and record your pulse again after 2, 4, and 6 minutes.

Results:

Predicted resting pulse	Actual resting pulse	Pulse after exercise			
		0 min.	2 min.	4 min.	6 min.

Conclusions:

How did your pulse rate change after you exercised? _____

_____

Why did this happen? _____

How long did it take for your pulse to go back to normal?_____

Did your pulse rate go back down as quickly as it went up? Explain. _____

_____

Name _____

Don't Miss the Boat!

Pretend that you are on a miniature submarine or a boat in the bloodstream of the human body. Begin your trip at a certain location in the body and write a travelogue, or traveler's journal, describing your voyage as you make a round-trip through the blood vessels, heart, lungs, and other parts of the body.

_____

_____

_____

_____

_____

_____

_____

_____

_____

_____

_____

_____

_____

_____

_____

_____

_____

Name _____

Researching the Circulatory System

Below is a list of common diseases or illnesses of the circulatory system. Choose one from the list to research. Use the information you find to answer the following questions.

anemia	heart attack	high blood pressure
leukemia	aneurysm	sickle-cell anemia
hemophilia	arteriosclerosis	rheumatic fever

Which disorder did you choose? _____

What is the cause of this disorder? _____

_____

_____

_____

How does this disorder affect the body? What are the symptoms?

_____

_____

_____

_____

What is the treatment for this disorder? _____

_____

_____

_____

_____

What other interesting facts did you learn? _____

_____

_____

_____

_____

References:_____

_____

_____

Name _____

KWL Chart
The Excretory System

The main function of the excretory system is to remove waste products from the body.

Before you begin learning about the excretory system, complete the first two sections of the chart below. Under **K**, list what you already know about the system. Under **W**, list what you would like to find out about the system. After you have studied the system, go back to the chart and list what you learned under **L**.

K What I know	W What I want to find out	L What I learned

Name _____

How the Excretory System Works

To find out what you already know about the excretory system, write a word or words from the Word Bank to complete each definition.

Word Bank

bladder	nephrons	kidneys	excretory system
urine	lungs	urethra	ureter skin

_____ 1. The function of the _____ is to excrete, or remove waste from the body.

_____ 2. When the body uses food for energy, carbon dioxide, water, and heat are produced as waste products. Carbon dioxide and water are given off when you exhale from the _____.

_____ 3. Heat is given off through the largest organ of the body, the _____.

_____ 4. As the body breaks down extra proteins, it forms a waste called urea. Salt is also given off as a waste product. Small amounts of urea and salt are released from the skin when you sweat, but most of it is released from the main organs of excretion in the body, the _____.

_____ 5. The two kidneys are at the back of the body, just above the hips. They form a liquid called _____ , which is made up of wastes and water.

_____ 6. Each kidney contains millions of tiny tubes called ___, which have capillaries wrapped around them. These tiny tubes filter and cleanse the blood and balance the supply of water and salt in the body.

_____ 7. Water from the blood goes into the nephrons along with urea, salt, and wastes. Urine forms from these waste products inside of the nephrons and then flows to a collecting area in the kidney. The urine leaves each kidney through a tube called the _____.

_____ 8. After leaving the kidney through the ureters, the urine is collected in a sac-like organ called the _____ , where it is stored until it is ready to be released from the body.

_____ 9. When urine is released from the body, it passes from the bladder through another tube called the _____ , which carries it out of the body.

Name _____

The Excretory System

Use the words from the Word Bank to label the diagram of the excretory system.

Word Bank

skin	lung	urethra
kidney	ureter	bladder

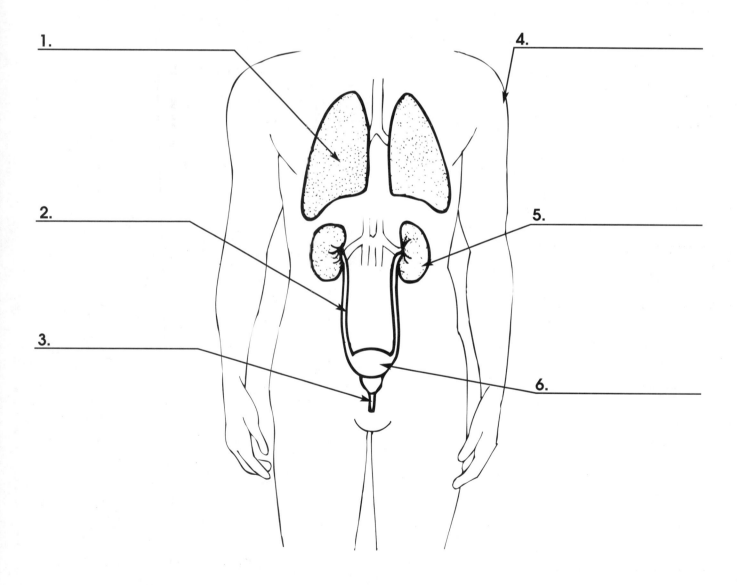

1. _____

2. _____

3. _____

4. _____

5. _____

6. _____

Name _____

Excretory Organs and Functions

Complete the crossword puzzle.

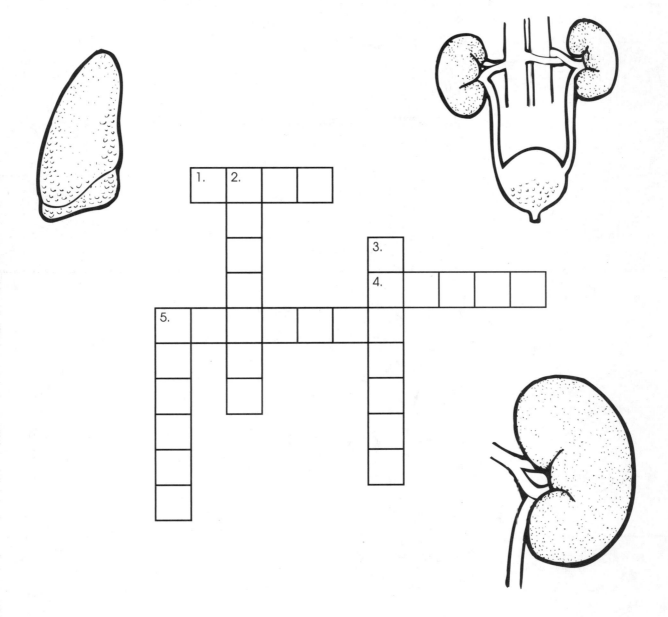

Across

1. removes water, salt, and body heat

4. remove water, carbon dioxide, and body heat; bring oxygen to your blood

5. a tube that leads out of the bladder and carries urine out of the body

Down

2. main organs of excretion; remove water and salt; produce urine

3. stores urine

5. a tube that carries urine out of the kidneys

Name _____

KWL Chart

The Endocrine System

The main function of the endocrine system is to help control the body through the release of chemicals called hormones.

Before you begin learning about the endocrine system, complete the first two sections of the chart below. Under **K**, list what you already know about the system. Under **W**, list what you would like to find out about the system. After you have studied the system, go back to the chart and list what you learned under **L**.

K What I know	W What I want to find out	L What I learned

Name _____

How the Endocrine System Works

To find out what you already know about the endocrine system, write a word or words from the Word Bank to complete each definition.

Word Bank

gland	hormones	endocrine system	parathyroid glands	testes
ovaries	pancreas	pituitary gland	adrenal gland	thyroid gland

_____ 1. The _____ is a system of the body that is made up of glands that release chemicals to control certain body functions.

_____ 2. Any organ that makes chemicals to control certain body functions is called a _____. Some glands release their chemicals through ducts, or tubes, while others release their chemicals directly into the blood.

_____ 3. The endocrine glands produce chemicals called _____. These are released into the blood.

_____ 4. The _____, or "master gland," is located at the base of the brain. It releases many different hormones that control other glands. It also releases a hormone that controls how the body grows.

_____ 5. The _____ releases hormones that help control the body's use of sugar and minerals. These glands also release a hormone called adrenaline, which helps the body to respond to stress, excitement, and exercise. This gland is located above each of the two kidneys.

_____ 6. The _____ is located in the neck. It makes a hormone that controls the rate at which the body uses energy.

_____ 7. The four glands known as the _____ are attached to the thyroid gland. They release a hormone that acts with another hormone released by the thyroid gland to control the amount of calcium and phosphorous in blood.

_____ 8. The gland located just under the stomach is called the _____. Part of this gland releases a chemical into a duct that is used in digestion. It also releases a hormone into the blood called insulin, which controls the amount of sugar, or glucose, in the blood.

_____ 9. The _____ are the female reproductive organs that release hormones to produce female characteristics and prepare the body for reproduction.

_____ 10. The male reproductive organs are the _____. They release hormones that produce male characteristics and prepare the body for reproduction.

Name _____

The Endocrine System

Use the words from the Word Bank to label the diagram of the endocrine system.

Word Bank

thyroid gland	pituitary gland	ovaries (female)
pancreas	testes (male)	adrenal glands
	parathyroid glands	

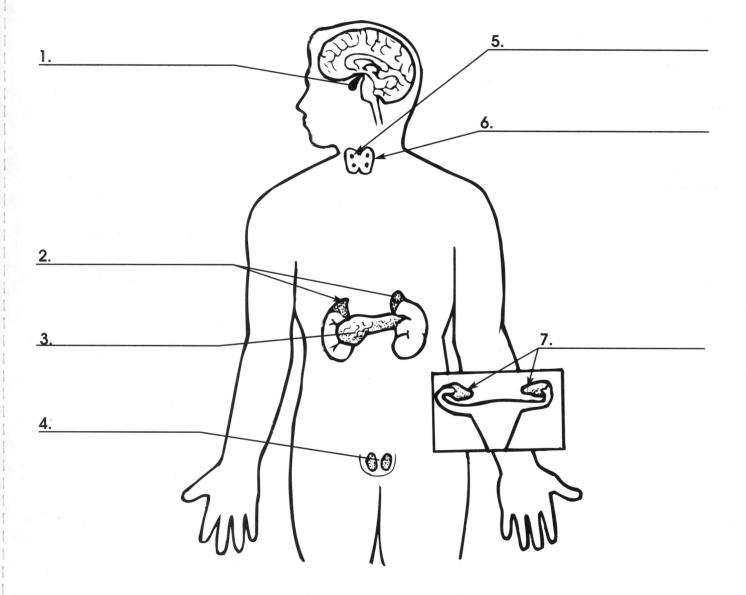

1. _____

5. _____

6. _____

2. _____

3. _____

7. _____

4. _____

Name _____

The Gland Finale

Unscramble the words and fill in the boxes.

1. the female reproductive organs that release hormones to produce female characteristics and prepare the body for reproduction

   vaiores

2. chemicals that are produced by glands and released into the blood

   honrmeso

3. the gland located just under the stomach that releases insulin and pancreatic juice

   aparescn

4. the system of the body that is made up of glands that release chemicals to control certain body functions

   dconeinre

5. the "master gland" located at the base of the brain which controls growth and releases many different hormones to control other glands

   itryaiput

6. the four glands that help control the amount of calcium and phosphorous in the blood

   atihrradoyp

7. the glands that release adrenaline to help the body respond to stress and exercise

   ldanera

8. the male reproductive organs that release hormones to produce male characteristics and prepare the body for reproduction

   setest

9. the gland in the neck that makes a hormone which controls the rate at which the body uses energy

   yrhdoit

Name _____

KWL Chart

The Nervous System

The main functions of the nervous system are to receive and carry messages throughout the body and to coordinate the parts of the body.

Before you begin learning about the nervous system, complete the first two sections of the chart below. Under **K**, list what you already know about the system. Under **W**, list what you would like to find out about the system. After you have studied the system, go back to the chart and list what you learned under **L**.

K What I know	W What I want to find out	L What I learned

Name _____

How the Nervous System Works

To find out what you already know about the nervous system, write a word or words from the Word Bank to complete each definition.

Word Bank

spinal cord	dendrites	association	impulse	nervous system
cerebellum	sensory	stimuli	axon	cerebrum
central	cell body	neurons	peripheral	brain
reflex	medulla	synapse	motor	

_____ 1. The ____ controls the body's reactions to the outside world. It is the system that controls the actions, emotions, thoughts, memories, sensations, and senses.

_____ 2. The nervous system collects information from inside and outside the body. It is triggered to respond to ____ , which are events or conditions that cause a living thing to react.

_____ 3. The nervous system is made up of ____ , or nerve cells, which carry messages throughout the body.

_____ 4. The main part of a neuron is called the ____ .

_____ 5. The cell body has many short strands branching out from it called ____ . These bring messages to the cell body.

_____ 6. The single, long strand that comes out of the other side of the cell body is called the ____ . This is the part of the neuron that carries messages away from the cell body.

_____ 7. The message that travels through the neuron is called an ____ . It can be received by one or more dendrites, and then it travels to the cell body and on to the axon. From the axon, the message moves to the next neuron.

_____ 8. Even though impulses move from neuron to neuron, they do not touch one another. Between two neurons, there is a gap called a ____ . This is the space between neurons where electrical and chemical signals jump from neuron to neuron.

_____ 9. There are three types of neurons. One type carries impulses toward the spinal cord and brain. These are called ____ neurons. When you pet a dog, this type of neuron carries the impulses from your fingers to your brain.

72

Name _____

_____ 10. Some neurons carry impulses from the brain or spinal cord out to other organs. These are called ____ neurons. This type of neuron can cause muscles to contract.

_____ 11. Some neurons serve as links, or connectors, between the sensory neurons and the motor neurons. These are found in the spinal cord or brain and are called ____ neurons.

_____ 12. The ____ , which is protected by the skull, is the main control center of the nervous system. In adults, it weighs about three pounds and is made up of billions of neurons.

_____ 13. The ____ is the structure that carries messages between the brain and the other parts of the body.

_____ 14. The brain and the spinal cord together make up what is known as the ____ nervous system. If a neuron in this part of the nervous system is damaged, it will not repair itself or regrow.

_____ 15. The brain has three main parts. The largest part of the brain is called the ____ . It is made up of a right half and a left half; each controls the opposite sides of the body. This is the part of the brain that controls learning, memory, and reasoning, and it also controls the muscles. Different regions of this part of the brain function in hearing, smelling, seeing, and touching.

_____ 16. The ____ is the part of the brain that controls balance, posture, complex movements, and muscle coordination.

_____ 17. The part of the brain that controls the functions necessary for life, such as heartbeat, breathing, and blood pressure is called the ____ . Other involuntary actions that are controlled by this part of the brain include coughing and sneezing.

_____ 18. The ____ nervous system is made up of the nerves that branch from the brain and spinal cord. It carries messages from the central nervous system to other parts of the body.

_____ 19. Some actions happen automatically and do not involve the brain. This type of action is called a ____ and is a quick, automatic response to a stimulus. An example of this would be a person automatically pulling his finger away after touching a hot stove.

Name _____

The Body's Control Center

The brain is the main control center of the nervous system.

Use the words from the Word Bank to label the parts of the brain.

Word Bank

cerebrum   cerebellum   spinal cord
medulla   brain stem

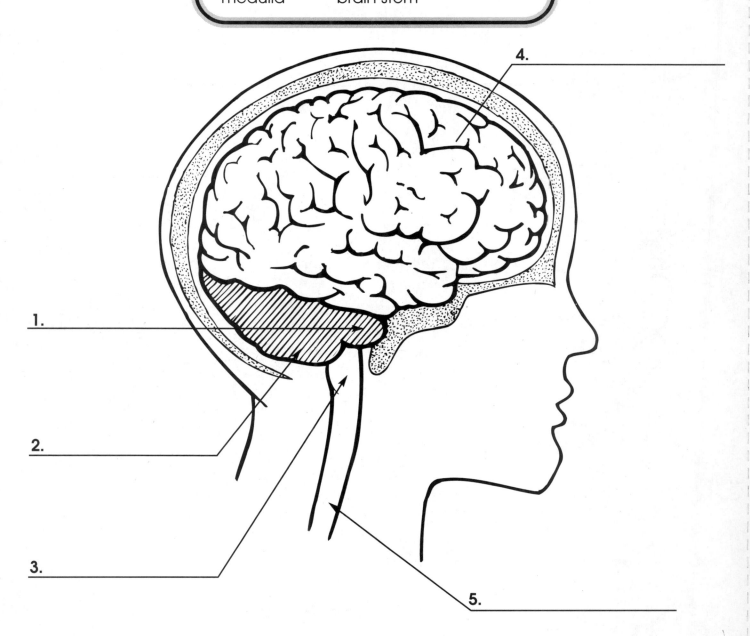

Name _____

Neurons

Neurons are nerve cells that carry messages throughout the body. The main part of a neuron is called the cell body. Many fibers lead out from the cell body. Some of these fibers are dendrites, which carry messages to the cell body. The long, single fiber that comes out from the other side of the cell body is called the axon. The axon carries messages away from the cell body.

Use the words from the Word Bank to label the parts of a neuron.

Word Bank

nucleus   cell body   axon endings

axon   dendrites

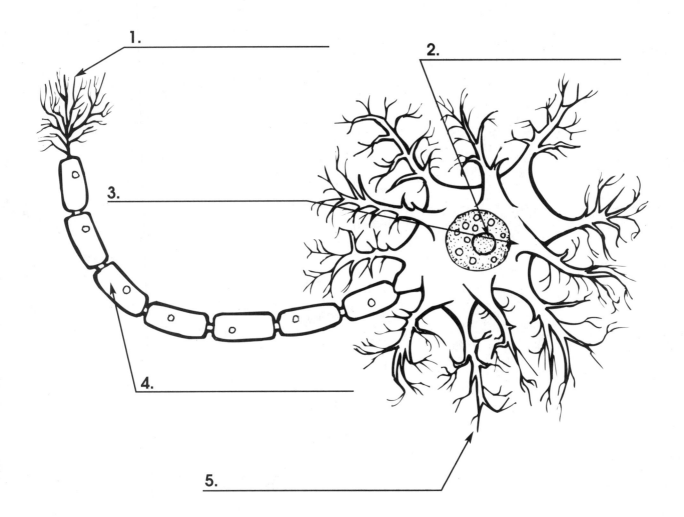

1. _____

2. _____

3. _____

4. _____

5. _____

Name _____

Job Descriptions

Write the letter of each function of the nervous system next to the part it describes. Then, draw a line from each function to the area in the picture it describes.

Function

a. I control thought, voluntary movement, memory, and learning. What am I?

b. I control balance and muscle coordination. What am I?

c. I carry messages between the spinal cord and body parts. What am I?

d. I relay messages between the brain and other parts of the body. What am I?

e. I control breathing, heartbeat, and other important functions. What am I?

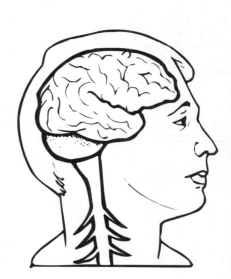

Parts

1. cerebellum _____

2. cerebrum _____

3. spinal cord _____

4. medulla _____

5. spinal nerve(s) _____

Code			
c = 1	e = 2	f = 3	i = 4
n = 5	p = 6	r = 7	t = 8
v = 9	w = 10	y = 11	

Use the code to fill in the blanks to complete the fascinating fact.

The brain needs lots of oxygen. It weighs about three pounds. That is about 1/50 of the

body's total adult weight. It uses __ __ __ __ __ __ - __ __ __ __
                                               8 10 2 5 8 11   3 4 9 2

__ __ __ __ __ __ __ of the oxygen the body takes in.
6 2 7 1 2 5 8

Name _____

A Brain Booster

Circle the words from the Word Bank in the puzzle. The words can be found horizontally, vertically, and diagonally.

Word Bank

axon	dendrites	spinal cord	sensory neurons
brain	cerebrum	motor neurons	association neurons
reflex	impulse	neuron	central nervous system
stimuli	cell body	cerebellum	peripheral nervous system
medulla	synapse	nervous system	

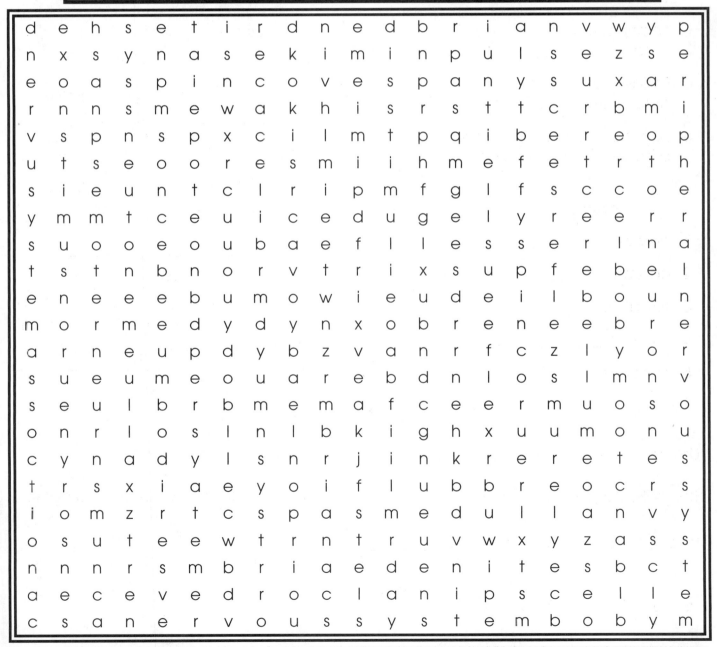

```
d e h s e t i r d n e d b r i a n v w y p
n x s y n a s e k i m i n p u l s e z s e
e o a s p i n c o v e s p a n y s u x a r
r n n s m e w a k h i s r s t t c r b m i
v s p n s p x c i l m t p q i b e r e o p
u t s e o o r e s m i i h m e f e t r t h
s i e u n t c l r i p m f g l f s c c o e
y m m t c e u i c e d u g e l y r e e r r
s u o o e o u b a e f l l e s s e r l n a
t s t n b n o r v t r i x s u p f e b e l
e n e e b u m o w i e u d e i l b o u n
m o r m e d y d y n x o b r e n e e b r e
a r n e u p d y b z v a n r f c z l y o r
s u e u m e o u a r e b d n l o s l m n v
s e u l b r b m e m a f c e e r m u o s o
o n r l o s l n l b k i g h x u u m o n u
c y n a d y l s n r j i n k r e r e t e s
t r s x i a e y o i f l u b b r e o c r s
i o m z r t c s p a s m e d u l l a n v y
o s u t e e w t r n t r u v w x y z a s s
n n n r s m b r i a e d e n i t e s b c t
a e c e v e d r o c l a n i p s c e l l e
c s a n e r v o u s s y s t e m b o b y m
```

77

Name _____

The Nervous System

Complete the crossword puzzle on page 79 using the clues below.

Across

2. a message that travels through a neuron

5. neurons that carry impulses toward the spinal cord and brain

6. the space between two neurons where electrical and chemical signals jump from neuron to neuron

8. carries messages from the central nervous system to other parts of the body

14. the main control center of the nervous system that is protected by the skull

17. the many short strands branching out from a neuron that carry messages to the cell body

18. the part of the brain that controls balance, posture, movement, and coordination

Down

1. the main part of a neuron

3. a single, long strand coming out of a neuron that carries messages away from the cell body

4. neurons that serve as links between the sensory neurons and the motor neurons

7. the largest part of the brain

9. an automatic action that does not involve the brain

10. the system of the body that controls the actions, emotions, thoughts, memories, sensations, and senses

11. structure that carries messages between the brain and other parts of the body

12. events or conditions that cause a living thing to react

13. neurons that carry impulses from the brain or spinal cord to other organs and cause muscles to contract

15. nerve cells that carry messages throughout the body

16. the part of the brain that controls breathing, heartbeat, and other functions necessary for life

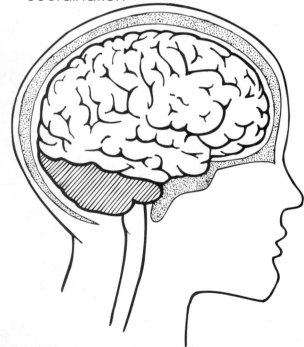

Name _____

The Nervous System

Name _____

Researching the Nervous System

Below is a list of common diseases or illnesses of the nervous system. Choose one from the list to research. Use the information you find to answer the following questions.

epilepsy	Alzheimer's	Parkinson's
meningitis	brain tumor	multiple sclerosis
stroke	poliomyelitis	paralysis

Which disorder did you choose? _____

What is the cause of this disorder? _____

_____

_____

_____

How does this disorder affect the body? What are the symptoms?

_____

_____

_____

_____

What is the treatment for this disorder? _____

_____

_____

_____

_____

What other interesting facts did you learn? _____

_____

_____

_____

References: _____

_____

_____

Name _____

KWL Chart
The Five Senses

Before you begin learning about the five senses, complete the first two sections of the chart below. Under **K**, list what you already know about the senses. Under **W**, list what you would like to find out about the senses. After you have studied the senses, go back to the chart and list what you learned under **L**.

K What I know	W What I want to find out	L What I learned

Name _____

Skin Deep

To find out what you already know about the human skin, write a word or words from the Word Bank to complete each definition.

Word Bank

oil glands	skin	hair follicles	epidermis	dermis
epithelial	melanin	sweat glands	pores	keratin

_____ 1. The _____ is the largest organ of the body.

_____ 2. Skin is made up of two layers that provide a protective covering for the body. The outer layer of the skin is called the _____.

_____ 3. The epidermis is made of _____ tissue and contains two kinds of cells.

_____ 4. The outer surface cells are either dead or are dying. Millions of these cells get rubbed off the body every day. These cells contain _____, which is a protein that makes the skin waterproof.

_____ 5. Living cells deep inside the epidermis contain _____, which is a brown pigment that colors the skin.

_____ 6. The inner, thicker layer of the skin is called the _____.

_____ 7. Most of the structures of the skin are found in the dermis. The dermis contains vessels, nerves, fat cells, glands, pores, and hair follicles. _____ cool the body by giving off sweat or perspiration.

_____ 8. This sweat is given off through openings called _____.

_____ 9. _____ are deep pockets from which hair grows.

_____ 10. _____ in the dermis are connected to the hair follicles. These glands produce oil which keeps the hair and skin soft.

Name _____

The Great Cover-Up

The largest organ of the body is the skin. Skin covers the whole body—even the inside of body openings such as the nose and mouth.

Use the words from the Word Bank to identify the layers and different structures in the human skin.

Word Bank

epidermis	dermis	nerve cells	hair follicle	pore
blood vessels	fat cells	oil gland	sweat gland	hair

1. _____

2. _____

3. _____

4. _____

5. _____

6. _____

7. _____

8. _____

9. _____

10. _____

Name _____

Sensing Heat and Cold

Your skin has receptors that can sense heat and cold, but reactions to temperatures are relative. This means that we often decide if something is hot or cold based on the temperature of our skin. For example, if you drink from a cold-water tap, it may seem warm compared to water from the refrigerator. However, if you took a bath in water of that same temperature, it would seem very cold.

? **Question:**
Can our skin receptors be "fooled" in sensing warm and cold? **?**

Materials Needed:
- 3 large bowls or buckets
- water

Procedures:

A. Fill one bowl with very warm water, one bowl with cold water, and one bowl with water at room temperature.

B. At the same time, put your right hand in the bowl with cold water and your left hand in the bowl with very warm water. Leave your hands in the bowls for a few minutes until you get used to the water temperatures.

C. Next, place both hands in the bowl of room-temperature water. Record what temperature you are sensing with each hand.

Results:

Describe how the sensation of warm or cold differed between your right hand and your left hand. _____

_____

Conclusions:

What does it mean to adapt to a certain temperature of water?_____

_____

How do you explain different sensations of hot and cold felt with each hand?

_____

_____

_____

Name _____

How the Sense of Sight Works

To find out what you already know about the sense of sight, write a word or words from the Word Bank to complete each definition.

Word Bank

rods	iris	retina
pupil	lens	optic nerve
cornea	cones	cerebrum

_____ 1. The transparent area in front of the eye that allows light to enter is called the ____ .

_____ 2. The ____ is the colored part of the eye located behind the cornea. It is a ring of muscles that contracts or relaxes in response to light, which causes the pupil to change size.

_____ 3. The opening in the middle of the iris that controls the amount of light entering the eye is called the ____ .

_____ 4. Light passes through the pupil to the ____ , which is a clear, flexible structure.

_____ 5. The lens focuses light onto the ____ , which is an area of receptor cells in the back of the eye.

_____ 6. There are two kinds of receptor cells in the retina. ____ are receptor cells that detect the presence or absence of light.

_____ 7. Receptors that allow you to see color are called ____, which function well only in bright light.

_____ 8. The ____ is made up of special nerve cells that are connected to the rods and cones.

_____ 9. Messages from the rods and cones travel along the optic nerve to the sight center of the ____ , where the message is interpreted.

Name _____

The Eyes Have It

Use the words from the Word Bank to label the parts of the eye in the diagrams. Some words will be used more than once.

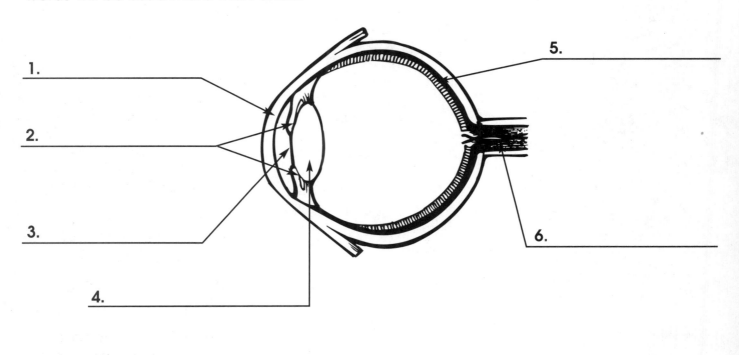

1. _____

2. _____

3. _____

4. _____

5. _____

6. _____

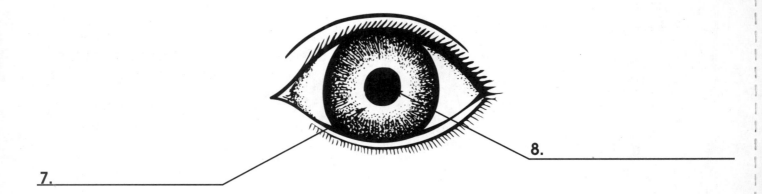

7. _____

8. _____

Word Bank

optic nerve	retina	cornea
lens	pupil	iris

Name _____

Seeing Is Believing

Match each word or words in List I with its description from List II. Write the number in the box of the matching letter. To discover the magic number, add a row, column, or diagonal. The answer should always be the same!

List I

_____ A. pupil

_____ B. lens

_____ C. iris

_____ D. cones

_____ E. retina

_____ F. optic nerve

_____ G. cornea

_____ H. rods

_____ I. cerebrum

List II

1. a clear, flexible structure that focuses light in the eye

2. part of the brain that controls learning, memory, and reasoning

3. receptor cells that are responsible for seeing color

4. the clear area in front of the eye

5. layer of receptor cells located at the back of the eye

6. colored part of the eye that contracts or relaxes in response to light

7. nerve that transmits messages from rods and cones

8. the opening in the iris whose size controls the amount of light entering the eye

9. receptor cells that detect the presence or absence of light

A	B	C
D	E	F
G	H	I

Magic Number

_____

Name _____

More Than Meets the Eye

Circle the words from the Word Bank in the puzzle. The words can be found horizontally, vertically, and diagonally.

```
e  s  i  r  i  s  i  g  t  c  o  r  n  h  a
e  l  a  s  h  e  y  e  l  a  s  h  p  p  l
y  r  o  d  e  s  d  u  r  o  s  h  u  x  e
c  e  p  p  c  o  n  e  h  e  y  p  p  b  n
o  t  e  u  t  g  t  y  n  y  i  l  l  l  n
t  b  t  p  z  i  e  o  c  l  f  e  i  i  s
c  a  h  i  n  y  c  a  b  d  e  n  p  n  n
u  n  g  a  t  c  o  n  e  c  h  s  u  k  e
d  g  i  r  e  e  o  h  e  o  p  u  p  i  r
r  c  s  d  o  y  g  r  p  r  b  i  i  n  v
a  o  p  t  t  i  e  r  h  n  v  l  e  r  h
e  d  d  i  l  e  y  e  d  e  l  e  n  o  e
t  s  s  i  g  b  t  a  k  a  c  o  p  d  y
b  t  e  a  r  d  u  c  k  r  o  o  d  s  c
```

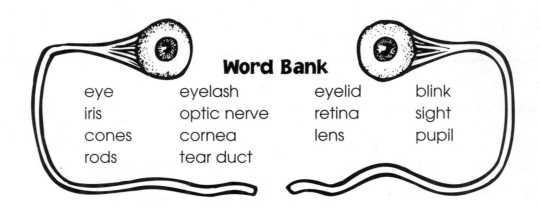

Word Bank

eye	eyelash	eyelid	blink
iris	optic nerve	retina	sight
cones	cornea	lens	pupil
rods	tear duct		

Name _____

Turn a Blind Eye

The eye has a blind spot, which is an area where no image can be seen at a certain distance. The blind spot is the area of the retina where the optic nerve leaves the eye, and there are no receptors present.

? **Question:**
Can you find a blind spot in your eye? **?**

Materials needed:
- •paper   •pencil   •ruler

Procedure:

A. Make an **X** in the middle of a piece of paper.

B. Make an **O** about 13 centimeters to the right of the **X**.

C. Hold the paper in front of you at arm's length and close your left eye.

D. Slowly move the paper toward you while you stare at the **X**. Keep your left eye closed and observe what happens to the **O**.

E. Close your right eye and look at the **O** from arm's length, then slowly bring the paper toward you and observe what happens to the **X**.

F. Repeat the experiment and have a partner measure the distance the paper is away from your eyes when the **X** or **O** disappears.

Results:

Describe what happened to the **O** as you moved the paper and kept your left eye closed. _____

Describe what happened to the **X** as you moved the paper and kept your right eye closed. _____

Distance paper is from eyes when X or O disappears	
left eye	**right eye**
_____	_____

Conclusions:

Did your eyes have a blind spot? Explain.

_____

Was the distance at which the **X** or **O** disappeared the same for both eyes? _____

How would you explain this?_____

Name _____

Sense of Sight

Complete the crossword puzzle.

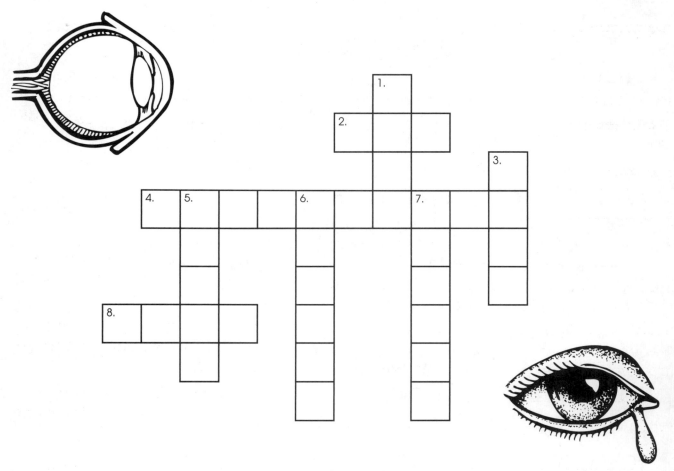

Across

2. receptor cell that detects the presence or absence of light and allows you to see dim light

4. a nerve that transmits messages from rods and cones

8. colored part of the eye that contracts or relaxes in response to light

Down

1. receptor cell that allows you to see color

3. a clear, flexible structure that focuses light in the eye

5. the opening in the iris whose size controls the amount of light entering the eye

6. the clear area in front of the eye

7. a layer of receptor cells at the back of the eye

Name _____

How the Sense of Hearing Works

To find out what you already know about the sense of hearing, write a word or words from the Word Bank to complete each definition.

Word Bank

eardrum	auditory canal	outer ear	cochlea	ear
middle ear	semicircular canals	auditory nerve	earwax	bones

_____ 1. The ____ is the organ of hearing and balance in humans.

_____ 2. The ____ , which is made up of two parts, gathers and funnels sound waves.

_____ 3. One part of the outer ear is the part of the ear you see. The other part is the ____ , which is an inch-long tube lined with hair.

_____ 4. The canal carries sound waves to the ____ , which is a round membrane that vibrates when sound waves hit it.

_____ 5. The canal also has cells that produce ____ , which stops the skin from drying out and protects the inner ear from dust and dirt.

_____ 6. The eardrum separates the outer ear from the ____ .

_____ 7. Vibrations of the eardrum pass through three tiny ____ in the middle ear called the anvil, the hammer, and the stirrup.

_____ 8. Inside the inner ear is the ____ , a coiled, fluid-filled tube that contains sound receptors.

_____ 9. These receptors send messages through the ____ to the hearing center of the brain.

_____ 10. Inside the inner ear, there are three ____ , which help the body keep its balance. These canals contain receptor cells and fluid. As the head moves, so does the fluid. The movement of the fluid causes the cells to send messages to the brain to control the balance.

Name _____

Now Hear This

Use the words from the Word Bank to label the parts of the ear.

Word Bank

auditory canal	semicircular canals	eustachian tube
auditory nerve	eardrum	cochlea
anvil	hammer	stirrup

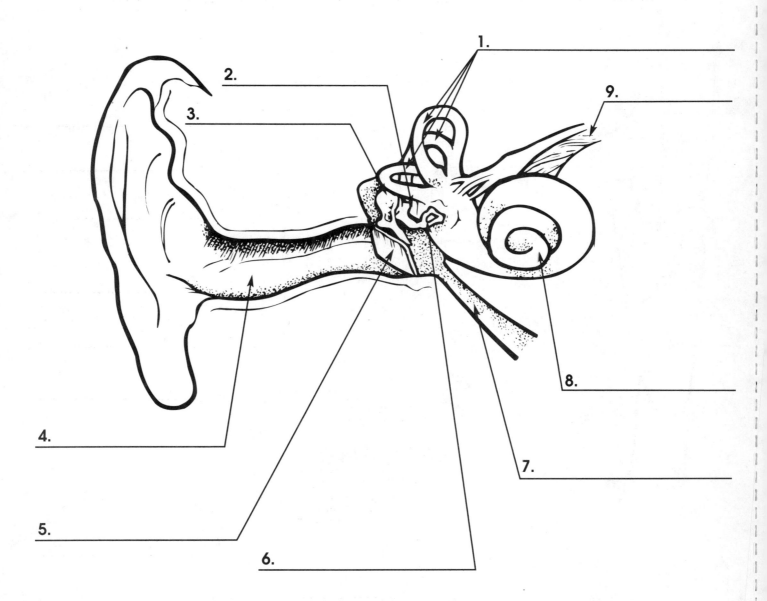

1.
2.
3.
4.
5.
6.
7.
8.
9.

Name _____

I'm All Ears

Use the words from the Word Bank to label the three major regions of the ear (outer ear, middle ear, and inner ear). Then, label the parts for each region.

Word Bank

eustachian tube	outer ear	middle ear	inner ear
auditory nerve	auditory canal	cochlea	stirrup
semicircular canals	eardrum	hammer	anvil

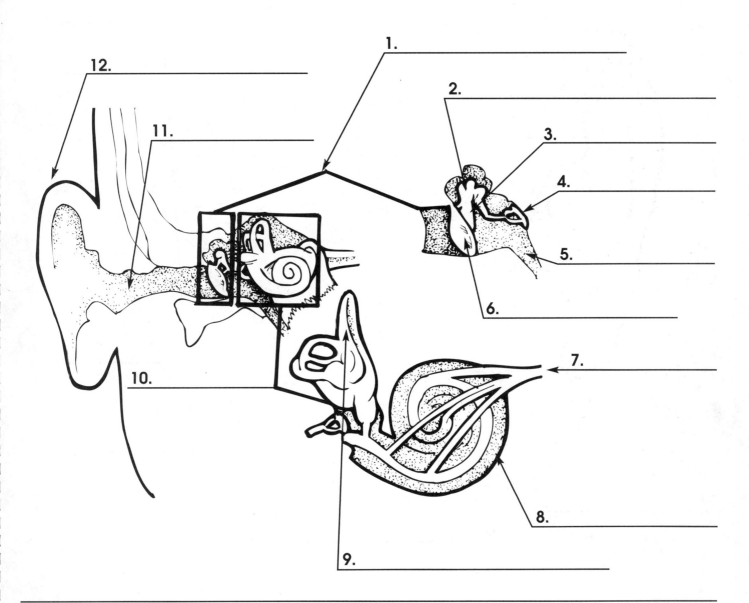

1. _____

2. _____

3. _____

4. _____

5. _____

6. _____

7. _____

8. _____

9. _____

10. _____

11. _____

12. _____

Name _____

Hear Ye! Hear Ye!

Match each word or words in List I with its description from List II. Write the number in the box of the matching letter. To discover the magic number, add a row, column, or diagonal. The answer should always be the same!

List I

____ A. outer ear

____ B. ear

____ C. cochlea

____ D. middle ear

____ E. earwax

____ F. eardrum

____ G. semicircular canals

____ H. auditory canal

____ I. auditory nerve

List II

2. the organ of hearing and balance

3. nerve that carries messages from the ear to the brain

4. contains three tiny bones: anvil, hammer, and stirrup

5. three canals containing fluid and cells to help the body maintain balance

6. sticky substance produced in the ear to protect the ear and keep the skin from drying out

7. a cciled, fluid-filled tube that contains sound receptors

8. a round membrane that vibrates when sound waves strike it

9. made up of the auditory canal and the part of the ear that is visible

10. a small tube lined with hair that makes up part of the outer ear

A	B	C
D	E	F
G	H	I

Magic number

_____

Name _____

Hammer It Out!

Circle the words from the Word Bank in the puzzle. The words can be found horizontally, vertically, and diagonally.

```
s  l  n  r  a  e  e  l  d  d  i  m  b  x  h
e  n  a  l  n  h  a  m  m  i  d  d  e  l  m
m  a  m  u  b  a  l  a  n  c  e  a  l  r  i
i  t  g  i  d  s  t  i  r  a  u  p  a  e  d
c  n  l  n  c  i  n  n  r  e  a  h  n  m  d
i  r  c  r  n  i  t  d  a  l  e  c  c  m  l
r  a  h  i  r  p  r  o  e  a  l  a  e  a  e
c  e  a  n  s  u  q  c  r  o  n  n  e  h  a
u  r  m  n  m  r  p  i  u  y  p  v  a  h  r
l  e  m  e  u  p  n  e  o  l  n  c  i  e  e
a  n  a  a  r  g  s  t  u  p  a  e  u  l  a
r  n  r  r  e  r  a  h  t  a  r  r  r  e  r
c  i  o  o  u  t  e  r  e  a  r  z  c  v  y
a  i  n  n  e  r  p  u  r  r  i  t  s  a  e
n  h  e  a  r  r  i  n  e  a  r  w  a  x  n
a  n  c  o  c  h  l  e  a  b  a  l  e  n  c
l  a  n  a  c  y  r  o  t  i  d  u  a  g  h
s  u  p  c  o  c  h  e  a  l  e  r  i  n  g
```

Word Bank

anvil	ear	inner ear
auditory canal	earwax	middle ear
auditory nerve	eardrum	outer ear
balance	hammer	semicircular canals
cochlea	hearing	stirrup

Name _____

How the Sense of Smell Works

To find out what you already know about the sense of smell, write a word or words from the Word Bank to complete each definition.

Word Bank

olfactory bulb	cilia	nostrils	receptor cells
nasal passages	mucus	cartilage	olfactory nerve

_____ 1. The nose, which is made of bone and flexible ____ , is the part of the breathing system that allows us to smell.

_____ 2. Air enters the nose through two openings called ____ .

_____ 3. From the nostrils, air passes into the ____ , which are tunnels inside the nose. These passages warm, moisten, and filter the air before it goes into the trachea and lungs so that the delicate lung tissue does not get damaged by the incoming air.

_____ 4. The airways are lined with a moist and sticky material called ____ , which helps to moisten the air and filter and trap dust and other particles in the air.

_____ 5. Inside of the nose are lots of tiny, curly hairs called ____ which also function in trapping particles from the air. The nasal passages are curved so that air flows and changes directions, allowing it to be better filtered, warmed, and moistened.

_____ 6. Scent molecules are invisible particles given off by smelly things. As you breathe in, some of these molecules enter the nose and reach the ____ .

_____ 7. Once they reach the receptors, the scent molecules send messages as electrical impulses through the ____ to the brain.

_____ 8. The impulses with the scent messages are interpreted in the brain in a section of the cerebrum behind the nose called the ____, where they register as smell.

Name _____

Don't Be Nosy!

Complete the crossword puzzle.

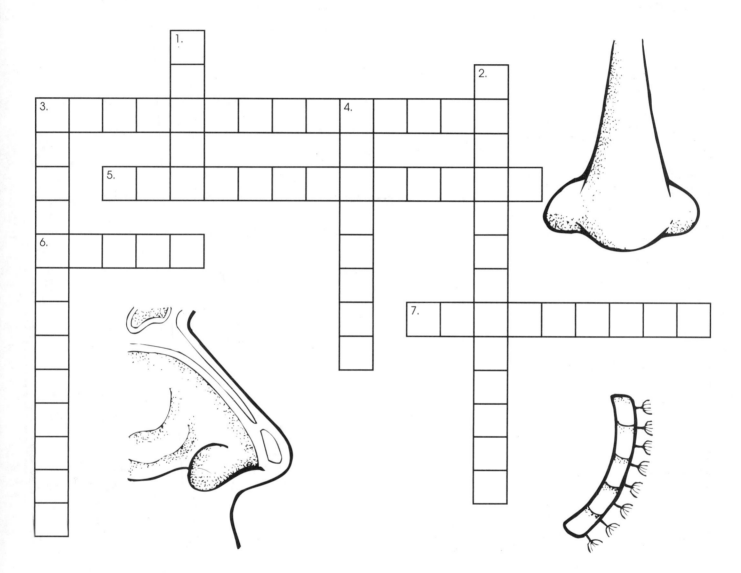

Across

3. sends scent messages to the brain

5. tunnels inside the nose that warm, moisten, and filter the air before it goes into the trachea

6. tiny hairs inside the nose

7. rubbery tissue making up the outer nose

Down

1. sticky substance inside the nose

2. cells in the nasal passages that pick up scent molecules

3. part of the brain where smell is interpreted

4. the openings of the nose

Name _____

Nosing Around

Circle the words from the Word Bank in the puzzle. The words can be found horizontally, vertically, and diagonally.

Word Bank

cartilage	nasal passages	olfactory bulb	receptor cells
cilia	nose	olfactory nerve	nostrils
	mucus	smell	

```
o  o  s  e  g  a  s  s  a  p  l  a  s  a  n
c  l  b  p  a  s  t  c  a  r  t  i  s  g  p
a  f  f  l  l  l  m  u  c  u  s  l  p  n  a
r  a  u  a  u  g  e  l  u  l  l  l  s  o  s
t  c  c  n  c  b  l  p  s  e  r  e  m  o  s
i  t  i  o  f  t  y  y  c  s  f  m  e  s  a
l  e  l  r  e  c  o  r  t  o  r  s  l  e  g
a  r  i  e  l  l  o  r  o  s  s  l  f  h  e
g  y  a  s  s  t  o  r  y  t  i  e  s  o  n
e  n  c  c  p  m  u  c  u  n  c  c  s  s  s
n  e  r  e  c  e  p  t  o  r  e  a  l  l  m
o  v  c  c  i  l  l  i  a  n  o  r  f  a  e
s  e  s  l  i  r  t  s  o  n  s  i  v  l  l
r  m  e  l  l  c  a  r  t  i  l  a  a  e  o
```

Name _____

The Nose Knows

Thousands of different odors can be identified with the sense of smell. Many animals communicate by using various scents to identify friends and enemies. In this activity, you will explore what it would be like to use your nose to find out who your friends are!

 Question:

Can you "follow your nose" to find a person that matches your scent?

Materials Needed:
- at least 8 participants
- cotton balls
- chalkboard or poster board
- small plastic vials with lids or film canisters (one per person)
- a variety of strongly scented liquid materials, such as room fresheners, perfumes, spices, or cleaning products that have scents such as pine, vanilla, lemon, etc.

Procedures:
A. For each of the liquid scents, put a small amount of liquid on two cotton balls and place each cotton ball in a canister or vial. Put the lid on the canisters until you begin the activity.

B. Prepare enough canisters for all the participants and distribute them randomly.

C. Tell each participant to open her canister and smell the scent. Then, have each participant try to locate the person who has the matching scent using only her sense of smell. No talking or gesturing is allowed.

D. Collect the canisters, redistribute them, and repeat the activity one or more times.

Results:
The first pair to match up their scents should write the name of their scent on the poster board or chalkboard.

Conclusions:
Were there some scents that were easier to match up than others? _____

_____

_____

What do you think are some of the factors that affect how quickly you found your match? _____

_____

Was it easier to find your match in the repeated trial after learning to use your nose in the first trial? Why? _____

_____

_____

Name _____

How the Sense of Taste Works

To find out what you already know about the sense of taste, write a word or words from the Word Bank to complete each definition.

Word Bank

receptor cells	taste buds	smell	sweet	salty
taste pores	tongue	sour	bitter	saliva

_____ 1. The organ that is used to taste is called the ____ .

_____ 2. The surface of the tongue is covered with several thousand receptors called ____ .

_____ 3. To taste something, the part of the food that carries the flavor must be dissolved in ____ , which is the digestive liquid released in the mouth.

_____ 4. As the food dissolves in the mouth, it enters openings in the taste buds called ____ .

_____ 5. Below each taste pore are ____ , which send signals to the brain's taste center, the place where tastes are identified.

_____ 6. There are four basic tastes that the tongue can recognize. Located on the tip of the tongue are the taste buds for ____ , or sugary flavors.

_____ 7. Located on the front sides of the tongue are the taste buds for foods that taste ____ , such as most crackers and potato chips.

_____ 8. Taste buds for foods that taste ____ , like lemon juice, are located on the back sides of the tongue.

_____ 9. Taste buds for substances that have a ____ taste, like baking soda, are located near the back of the tongue.

_____ 10. The sense of taste and ____ are closely linked because air enters from the nose and goes into the back of the throat, making it possible for us to taste a very strong odor that we inhale.

Name _____

A Tasty Puzzle

Circle the words from the Word Bank in the puzzle. The words can be found horizontally, vertically, and diagonally.

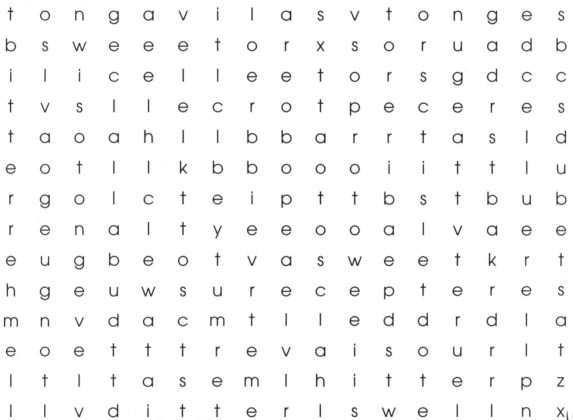

```
t o n g a v i l a s v t o n g e s
b s w e e e t o r x s o r u a d b
i l i c e l l e e t o r s g d c c
t v s l l e c r o t p e c e r e s
t a o a h l l b b a r r t a s l d
e o t l l k b b o o o i i t l u
r g o l c t e i p t t b s t b u b
r e n a l t y e e o o a l v a e e
e u g b e o t v a s w e e t k r t
h g e u w s u r e c e p t e r e s
m n v d a c m t l l e d d r d l a
e o e t t t r e v a i s o u r l t
l t l t a s e m l h i t t e r p z
l l v d i t t e r l s w e l l n x
```

Word Bank

bitter	salty	sweet	taste pores
receptor cells	smell	taste buds	tongue
	saliva	sour	

Name _____

You've Got Good Taste

Complete the crossword puzzle.

Across

2. thousands of receptors that cover the tongue

3. taste sensation produced by foods like potato chips

5. cells that send taste sensations to the brain

8. taste sensation produced by substances such as baking soda

Down

1. openings in the taste buds

3. taste sensation produced by sugary foods

4. digestive liquid released in the mouth that dissolves food

6. organ used for tasting

7. taste sensation produced by foods such as lemons

Name _____

Senses of Smell and Taste

Use the words from the Word Bank to label the structures that make up the sense organs for smell and taste. Then, label the sense areas of the tongue.

Word Bank

nasal passage	nostril	salty	bitter
olfactory nerve	brain	sweet	sour

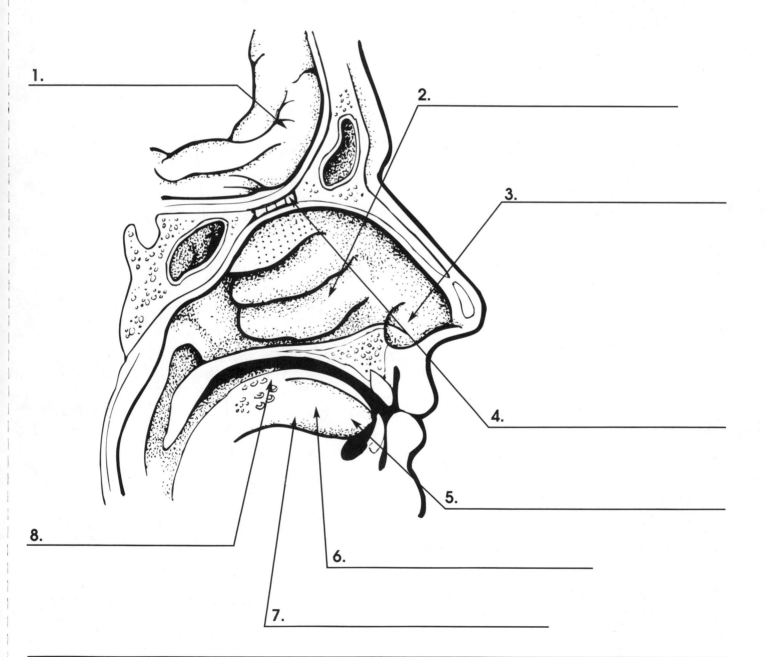

1. _____

2. _____

3. _____

4. _____

5. _____

6. _____

7. _____

8. _____

Name _____

A Map of the Tongue

The tongue is the sense organ for taste. The upper surface of the tongue is covered with little bumps called papillae. The surface of the tongue also has thousands of taste buds for determining if food tastes sweet, salty, sour, or bitter.

?   **Question:**   **?**
Can you locate the areas on your tongue that are sensitive to each of the four different tastes?

Materials Needed:
- cotton swabs
- lemon juice
- sugar water
- saltwater
- baking soda mixed with water
- plain water for rinsing

Procedures:

A. Work with a partner. Dip a cotton swab in sugar water and gently touch the swab on your partner's tongue, one spot at a time, until you have covered the entire surface.

B. On the map of the tongue, label each place as sweet where your partner tastes the sugar water.

C. Have your partner rinse out his mouth well with water. Use a clean swab to repeat the procedures for salty water (salty), baking soda water (bitter), and finally, lemon juice (sour).

Results:

Conclusions:

Is the entire tongue equally sensitive to each of the flavors? Explain.

_____

_____

_____

Are there some areas for detecting tastes that seem to overlap? If so, describe where.

_____

_____

How do you think we can taste so many different flavors if our taste buds are only sensitive to four different tastes?

_____

_____

Name _____

What's That Memory I Smell?

Did you know that the sense of smell is closely linked with memory? Sometimes a certain odor can trigger a particular memory. Scientists have found that the part of the brain that interprets smell is closely connected to the part of the brain that stores memories.

Concentrate on one of your favorite memories. Try to think of the smells involved with the particular event that you recall. Write a paragraph describing everything that you can remember about the event, especially the smells. Share your memory with a partner or with the class, and discuss what you commonly think of when you smell a particular scent. Do you think people with a better sense of smell are also better at remembering things?

_____

_____

_____

_____

_____

_____

_____

_____

_____

_____

_____

_____

_____

Name _____

Stimulating Those Senses

For each stimulus listed below, write the name of the sense organ that would be stimulated. Then, write a description of the sensation.

1. a dill pickle _____

_____

_____

_____

2. thunder _____

_____

3. molecules of skunk musk _____

_____

4. cactus needles _____

_____

5. lightning_____

_____

6. a balloon bursting _____

_____

7. lemon drops_____

_____

8. a shadow _____

_____

9. freshly baked bread _____

_____

10. a sharp needle _____

_____

Name _____

Some Handy Tips for Hand Washing

Some kinds of bacteria that live on skin can cause disease. Keeping your hands as clean as possible can help prevent you from getting sick. Because bacteria and dirt do not dissolve in water, soap is very important in the cleaning process. Soap helps the water penetrate the tiny folds and crevices in our skin to pick up dirt and microorganisms. Soap also helps to dissolve oil and grease so it can be carried away by the water.

Trace your hand in the box below. Next, draw some of the lines showing the location of creases and wrinkles. Use a red marker to put Xs on all the places of your traced hand that you think microorganisms such as bacteria would grow the best. Use a blue marker to put Os on the places of your traced hand to show the places where it would be the most difficult for microorganisms to grow.

When you wash your hands, remember to wash all of those places, especially the ones that you have marked with Xs. Practice washing your hands by following the steps listed below.

Hand-Washing Instructions

1. Wet your hands with warm water.
2. Rub your hands with soap.
3. Continue rubbing your hands together in a circular motion for about 30 seconds.
4. Clean under your fingernails and rub the areas between your fingers.
5. Rinse your hands with water, holding them with the fingers pointing downward.
6. Dry your hands well with a clean towel or air dryer.

Name _____

Eating Healthy

Eating the right foods in the right amounts is very important in keeping the body healthy and all organs and systems functioning properly. The food pyramid is a guide that shows information about the basic food groups and the number of servings that are recommended from each group on a daily basis.

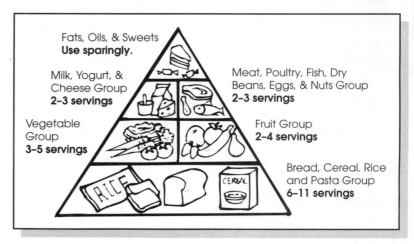

Study the food guide and the types of foods found in each food group. Notice the number of servings that are recommended from each group per day. Using the guide, plan three meals a day for three days that include the adequate number of servings from each group per day.

Day 1	Day 2	Day 3
Breakfast	Breakfast	Breakfast
Lunch	Lunch	Lunch
Dinner	Dinner	Dinner
Total for each group	Total for each group	Total for each group

Name _____

Healthy Essentials

Match each word or words in List I with its description from List II. Write the number in the box of the matching letter. To discover the magic number, add a row, column, or diagonal. The answer should always be the same!

List I

___ A. nutrients

___ B. proteins

___ C. carbohydrates

___ D. vitamins

___ E. minerals

___ F. fats

___ G. water

___ H. RDA

___ I. fiber

List II

1. recommended daily allowance

2. nourishment for the body

3. found in oily and greasy foods; help maintain healthy skin and hair

4. provides energy; can be found in starchy foods

5. build strong bones and teeth; can be found in all food groups

6. makes up over half of the body's weight; carries nutrients throughout the body and helps remove waste

7. help the body get energy from other nutrients

8. roughage; vegetables and whole grains are a good source of this

9. the body's building materials; found in milk, meat, and peanuts

A.	B.	C.
D.	E.	F.
G.	H.	I.

Magic Number

_____

Name _____

Product Information

Read the label on a food of your choice (breakfast cereal, frozen pizza, etc.). Use the information from the label to answer the questions.

1. What is the main ingredient in the food? _____

_____

2. What is the serving size for the food? _____

_____

3. How many calories are in one serving of the food? _____

_____

4. How much protein is in one serving of the food? _____

_____

5. How much calcium is in one serving of the food? _____

_____

6. How many vitamins and minerals does one serving of the food have? List them.

_____

_____

_____

_____

7. How many carbohydrates are in one serving of the food? _____

8. How much fat is in one serving of the food? _____

9. How much cholesterol is in one serving of the food? _____

_____

10. In what food group can the food be found? _____

_____

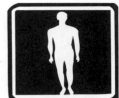

Name _____

Healthy Hunting

Circle the words from the Word Bank in the puzzle. The words can be found horizontally, vertically, and diagonally.

c	c	g	r	a	n	s	m	l	n	e	r	a	l	v
a	f	a	t	s	v	h	w	i	v	f	d	h	s	e
m	s	i	r	w	a	t	e	r	e	r	a	e	t	g
i	n	n	a	b	r	t	k	a	g	u	i	a	n	e
n	i	s	t	f	o	r	n	t	l	i	r	l	e	t
e	m	n	e	r	r	h	z	u	a	t	y	l	i	a
r	a	o	p	e	o	u	y	p	t	s	h	y	r	b
a	t	i	r	b	x	o	l	d	b	f	g	y	t	l
l	i	t	o	i	f	o	o	d	r	e	e	r	u	e
s	v	i	w	f	a	t	t	u	t	a	g	n	n	s
d	g	r	a	i	n	s	i	e	n	t	t	h	t	s
a	w	t	t	f	i	t	r	e	n	u	t	e	n	t
r	a	u	r	o	s	u	t	r	i	e	n	t	s	p
y	t	n	e	f	o	o	d	g	r	o	u	p	s	o

Word Bank

carbohydrates	food groups	minerals	vegetables
dairy	fruits	nutrients	vitamins
fats	grains	nutrition	water
fiber	healthy	protein	

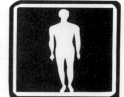

Name _____

Writing a Cinquain Poem

A cinquain is a non-rhyming poem that has five lines. Follow the instructions below to write a cinquain poem about a major organ of the body. When you have completed the poem, cut a piece of colored construction paper into the shape of the organ you have chosen. Cut out the poem and paste it on the construction paper background to hang in your classroom.

Line 1:   one word; the name of an organ (noun)

Line 2:   two words that describe line 1 (adjectives)

LIne 3:   three words; an action that your organ performs (verbs)

Line 4:   four words; a feeling about line 1

Line 5:   one word; a synonym or a word referring back to line 1 (noun)

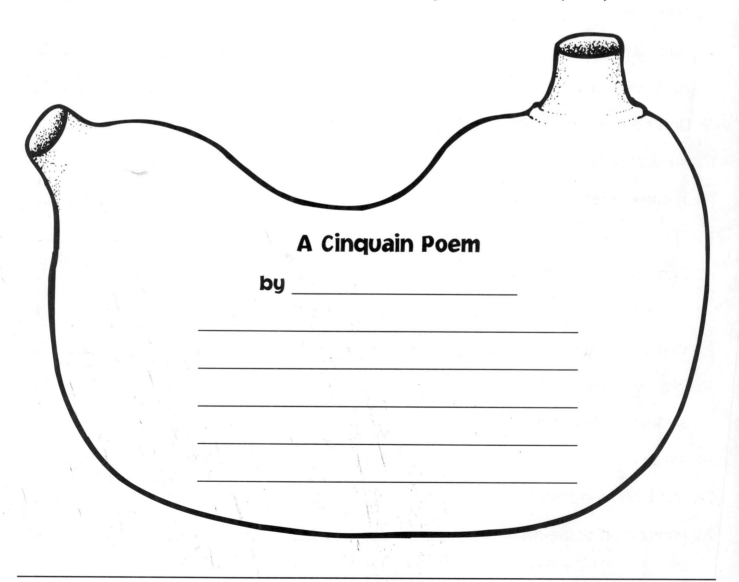

A Cinquain Poem

by _____

_____

_____

_____

_____

_____

Human Body: Grades 4–6

Name _____

Off the Top of Your Head

An idiom is an expression whose meaning is different from the literal meaning. Below are idioms or phrases that use names of body parts. Give the meaning of each phrase.

1. Lend me a hand. _____

2. You're pulling my leg. _____

3. Head and shoulders above the rest _____

4. I have a bone to pick with you. _____

5. Don't bite the hand that feeds you. _____

6. Break a leg! _____

7. He's all thumbs! _____

8. Put your heart into it. _____

9. Don't be an egghead! _____

10. An eye for an eye _____

11. In one ear and out the other _____

12. Put your foot down. _____

13. Don't put your foot in your mouth! _____

14. I'm getting cold feet. _____

15. Wet behind the ears _____

16. Wear your heart on your sleeve. _____

17. Stick your neck out! _____

18. Shake a leg! _____

19. The shoe is on the other foot. _____

20. Running off at the mouth _____

Name _____

More Human Body Idioms

An idiom is an expression whose meaning is different from the literal meaning. Below are idioms or phrases that use names of body parts. Give the meaning of each phrase.

1. I'm all ears! _____

2. Apple of my eye _____

3. Bite your tongue! _____

4. Blood is thicker than water. _____

5. Off the top of your head _____

6. More than meets the eye _____

7. Make no bones about it. _____

8. Lead you around by the nose _____

9. Keep your nose to the grindstone. _____

10. Keep your fingers crossed. _____

11. Head in the clouds _____

12. Get your feet wet. _____

13. Eyes in the back of your head _____

14. Egg on your face _____

15. Cost an arm and a leg _____

16. Put your best foot forward. _____

17. Keep a stiff upper lip. _____

18. No skin off my nose _____

19. Take a hard-nosed position. _____

20. Keep your head above water. _____

Name _____

Human Body Analogies

Analogies are comparisons of two sets of words. Complete each analogy with a word that names a body part.

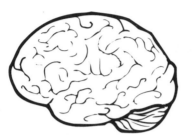 

1. Finger is to hand as _____ is to foot.

2. Knee is to leg as _____ is to arm.

3. Wrist is to hand as _____ is to foot.

4. A hearing aid is to ears as glasses are to _____ .

5. See is to eye as smell is to _____ .

6. Sock is to foot as glove is to _____ .

7. Hearing is to ear as seeing is to _____

8. Odor is to nose as sound is to _____ .

9. Tear is to eye as sweat is to _____ .

10. Shoulder is to arm as hip is to _____ .

11. Brain is to skull as lungs are to _____ .

12. Eardrum is to ear as retina is to _____ .

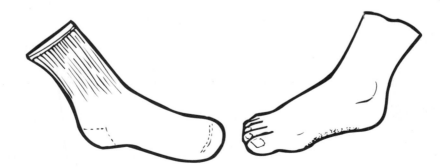

Name _____

I Don't Belong Here

There are many organs of the body, and each organ has a specific function. Organs work together to form systems.

There are four organs or body parts listed for each system below. Three of the body parts belong to that system; one does not. Cross out the body part that does not belong in each system.

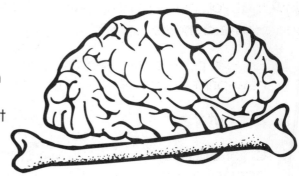

1. nervous system

   nerves   liver   spinal cord   brain

2. respiratory system

   diaphragm   lungs   trachea   pancreas

3. endocrine system

   heart   ovary   pituitary gland   thyroid gland

4. digestive system

   stomach   ribs   small intestine   esophagus

5. excretory system

   kidney   skull   bladder   urethra

6. skeletal system

   ligaments   bones   skull   cerebellum

7. circulatory system

   arteries   heart   veins   pharynx

8. muscular system

   gall bladder   tendons   muscles   biceps

Name _____

A Body Makeover

Now that you have studied the systems of the body and the organs they contain, you can create a model of your body and the organs inside. Follow the steps below.

1. Have a partner trace a complete outline of your body on large butcher or newsprint paper. Go over the pencil markings with a black marker.

2. Cut out the outline of your body.

3. Color and cut out the pictures of the organs of the body on pages 118–123. On the back of each organ, write the following:

   A) the name of the organ

   B) the name of the system of the body to which the organ belongs

   C) the function of the organ

4. Place the organs in the proper positions on the outline of your body. Glue the tabs down to keep the organs in place.

5. Quiz yourself or your partner by identifying each organ, the system of the body to which it belongs, and its function in the body.

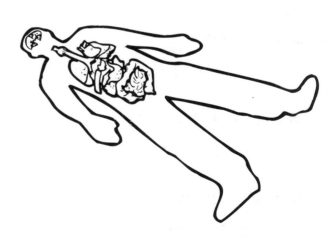

Name _____

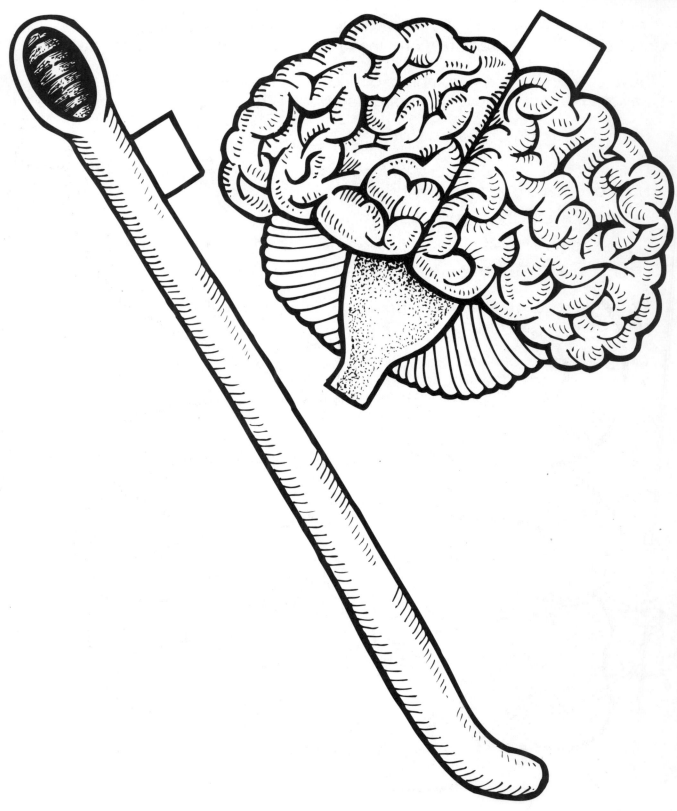

Name _____

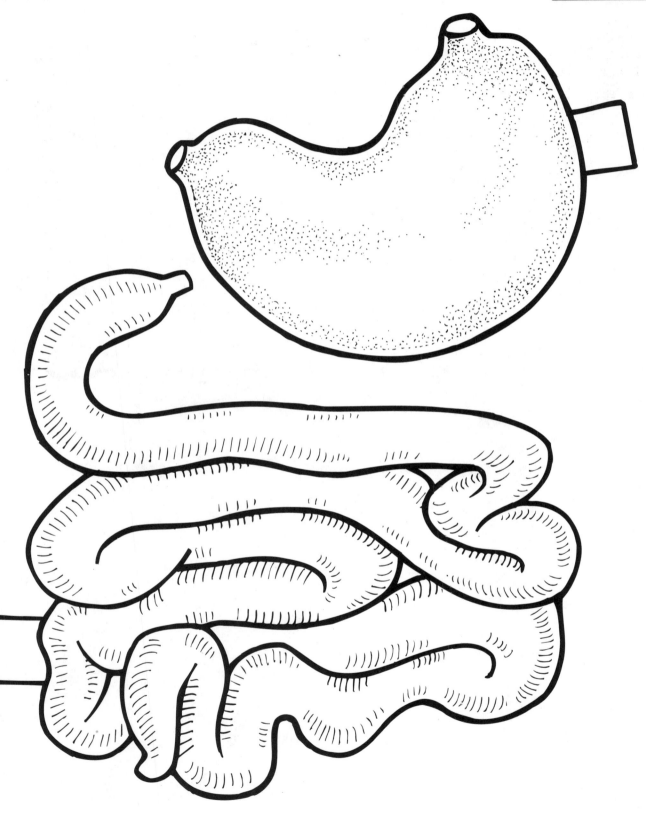

Name _____

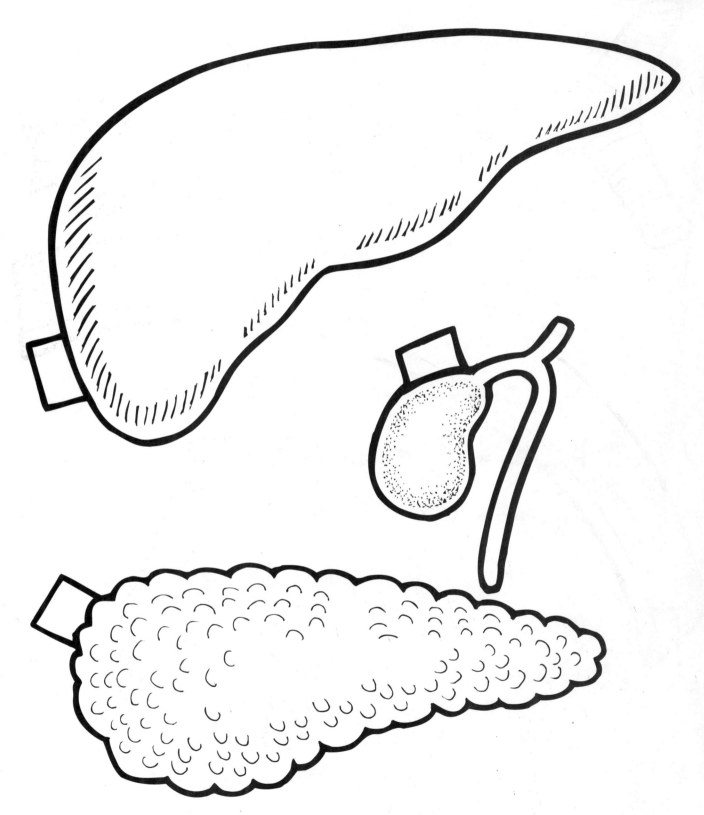

Name _____

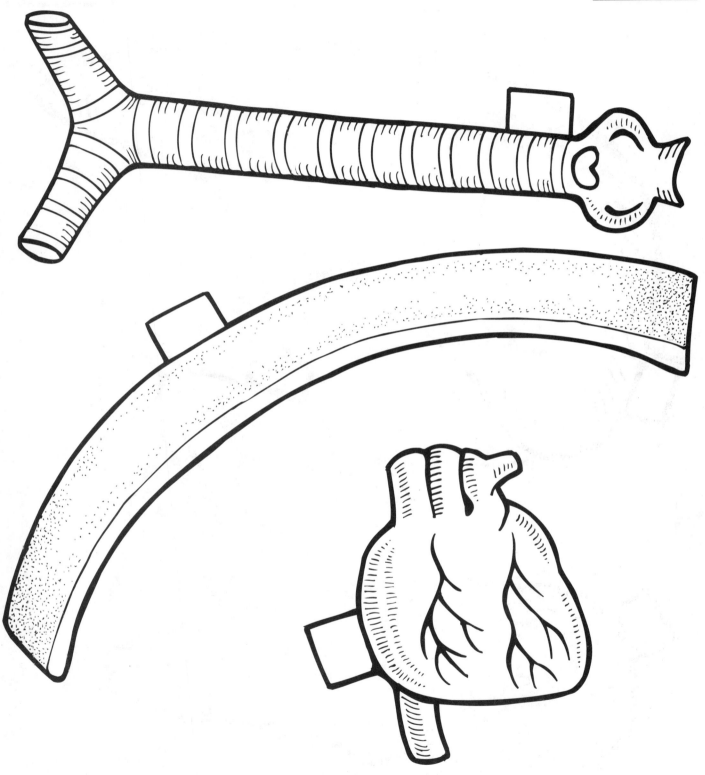

Name _____

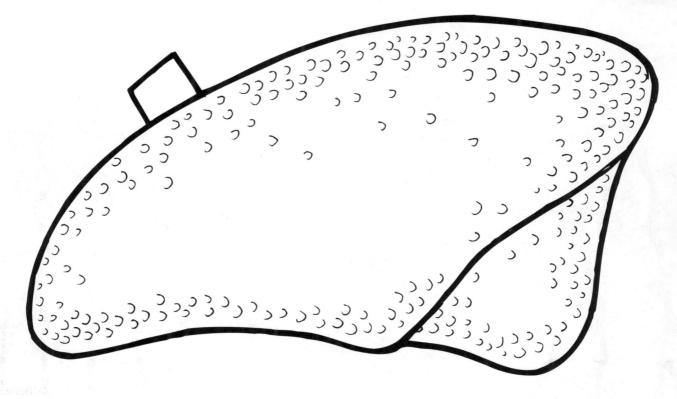

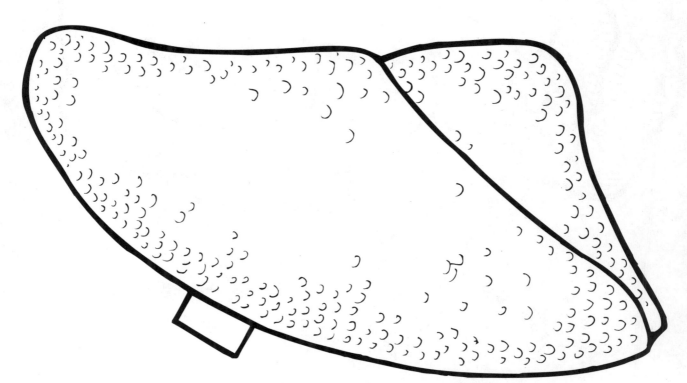

Name _____

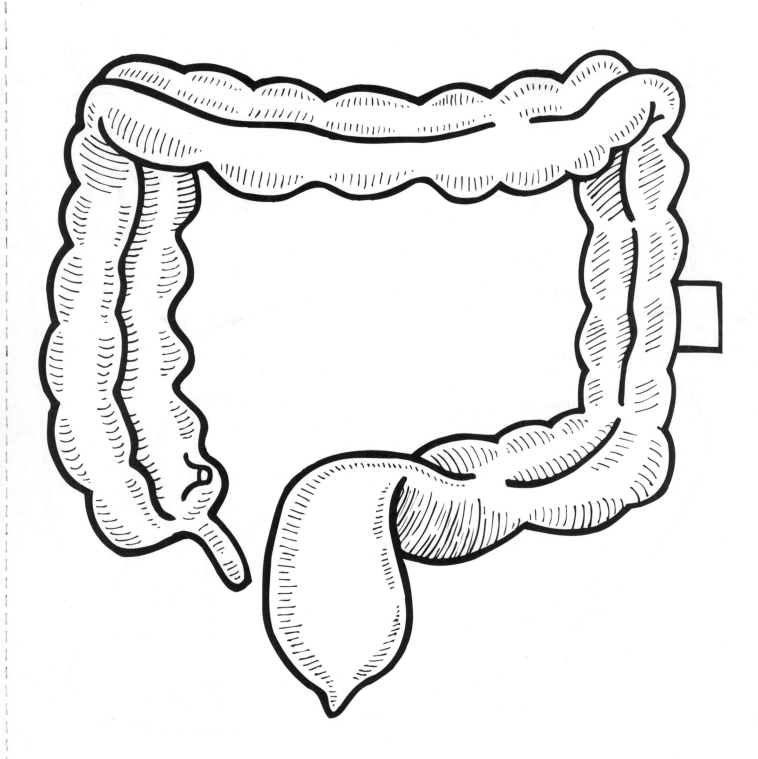

Answer Key

Page 4
1. bone cell; 2. muscle cell;
3. epithelial cell; 4. white blood cell;
5. red blood cell; 6. nerve cell

Page 5
Skeletal System: bones, ligaments, joints; Muscular System: muscles, tendons; Digestive System: liver, small intestine, stomach, esophagus, pancreas; Nervous System: brain, nerves, spinal cord; Circulatory System: blood vessels, heart; Respiratory System: diaphragm, lungs, trachea; Endocrine System: adrenal glands, thyroid gland, pituitary gland; Excretory System: bladder, urethra, kidney, ureter

Page 6
1. skeletal; 2. muscular; 3. digestive;
4. respiratory; 5. excretory;
6. endocrine; 7. circulatory;
8. nervous

Page 7
Charts will vary.

Pages 8–9
1. skeletal system; 2. bones;
3. cartilage; 4. joints; 5. fixed;
6. partially moveable; 7. moveable;
8. ligaments; 9. short; 10. hinge;
11. ball-and-socket; 12. pivot;
13. marrow; 14. calcium;
15. calcification; 16. long; 17. flat;
18. gliding; 19. irregular; 20. fracture

Page 10
1. cervical; 2. thoracic; 3. lumbar;
4. sacral; 5. coccygeal

Page 11
1. mandible; 2. clavicle; 3. humerus;
4. pelvis; 5. radius; 6. ulna;
7. phalanges; 8. cranium; 9. scapula;
10. rib cage; 11. vertebrae;
12. carpals; 13. femur; 14. patella;
15. tibia; 16. fibula; 17. tarsals

Page 12
1. humerus; 2. ulna; 3. clavicle;
4. scapula; 5. radius

Page 13
1. pelvis; 2. coccyx; 3. femur;
4. fibula; 5. lumbar vertebrae;
6. patella; 7. tibia

Page 14
1. phalanges; 2. metacarpal;
3. carpal; 4. tarsal; 5. metatarsals;
6. phalanges

Page 15
1. jawbone; 2. ribs; 3. hipbone;
4. finger bones; 5. kneecap; 6. skull;
7. arm bone; 8. backbone;
9. thighbone; 10. foot bones

Page 16
1. fixed; 2. ball-and-socket; 3. hinge;
4. gliding

Page 17
1. C2; 2. C2; 3. B; 4. A; 5. C4; 6. C3;
7. C1; 8. C1

Page 18

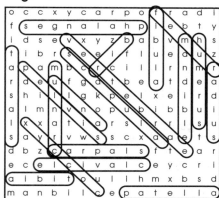

Page 19
Possible answers: 1. The bone with calcium is strong and cannot be bent. The bone soaked in vinegar has lost its calcium, so it feels softer and is more easily bent.; 2. Calcium is stored in bones and helps make bones hard and strong.; 3. A diet low in calcium can cause rickets, a disease in which bones become soft and easily bent. Low calcium can also cause osteoporosis, where bones lose their strength and can be easily broken.

Page 20
Charts will vary.

Pages 21–22
1. muscular system; 2. voluntary muscles; 3. involuntary muscles;
4. muscle tissue; 5. skeletal muscle;
6. smooth muscle; 7. cardiac muscle; 8. muscle cells; 9. tendons;
10. flexor; 11. extensor; 12. exercise;
13. strain; 14. cramp

Page 23
1. skeletal—attached to the skeleton (i.e. muscle in the legs, arms, back, etc.); 2. smooth—found in the walls of many organs and blood vessels;
3. cardiac—found in the heart

Page 24
1. contracts; 2. relaxes; 3. bicep;
4. tricep

Page 25

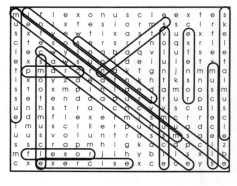

Page 26

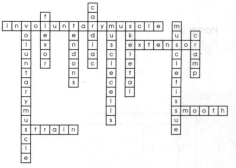

Page 27
Answers will vary. The student should be able to do fewer finger lifts each time. Lactic acid builds up in the finger muscles during exercise, and the muscle tires.

Page 28
Results: 1. yes; 2. no; 3. yes; 4. no;
5. no; 6. no; 7. Answers will vary.;
8. yes; 9. yes; 10. Answers will vary.;
11. yes; 12. yes
Conclusions: 1. voluntary;
2. involuntary; 3. both;
4. both; 5. voluntary; 6. involuntary

Page 29
Answers will vary.

Page 30
Charts will vary.

Answer Key

Pages 31–32
1. digestion; 2. mechanical;
3. chemical; 4. salivary glands;
5. saliva; 6. enzymes; 7. tongue;
8. esophagus; 9. peristalsis;
10. stomach; 11. gastric juice;
12. small intestine; 13. bile;
14. gallbladder; 15. pancreas;
16. intestinal juice; 17. villi; 18. large
intestine; 19. appendix; 20. rectum

Page 33
1. salivary glands; 2. liver;
3. gallbladder; 4. large intestine;
5. small intestine; 6. mouth;
7. esophagus; 8. stomach;
9. pancreas; 10. rectum

Page 34
1. crown; 2. root; 3. enamel;
4. dentin; 5. gums; 6. pulp; 7. bone;
8. cementum

Page 35
1. molars; 2. incisors; 3. premolars;
4. canines; 5. molars; 6. premolars;
7. canines; 8. incisors; 9. molars;
10. premolars; 11. canines; 12. incisors

Page 36
A.16; B. 10; C. 4; D. 9; E. 8; F. 5; G. 11;
H. 15; I. 13; J. 17; K. 6; L. 3; M. 2; N. 7;
O. 18; P. 12 Magic Number = 39

Page 37
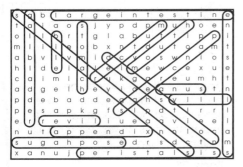

Page 38
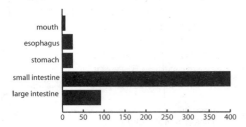

1. mouth; 2. esophagus; 3. stomach;
4. small intestine; 5. large intestine

Page 39
Results: yes; Descriptions will vary.
Conclusion: The cracker eventually
tasted sweet. Amylase from the
saliva breaks down the starch into
sugar. Saliva moistens food so it
can be swallowed more easily.
Saliva also contains some enzymes
that allow chemical digestion to
begin in the mouth.

Page 40
Results: Answers will vary.
Descriptions will vary.
Conclusion: Papain helps digest
proteins by chemically breaking
them down into substances that
can more readily be used by the
body.

Page 41
Stories will vary.

Page 42
Answers will vary.

Page 43
Answers will vary.

Page 44
Charts will vary.

Pages 45–46
1. respiratory system; 2. nose;
3. pharynx; 4. larynx; 5. vocal cords.
6. epiglottis; 7. trachea; 8. bronchi;
9. alveoli; 10. capillaries;
11. oxygen; 12. carbon dioxide;
13. diaphragm; 14. inhale;
15. exhale

Page 47
1. pharynx; 2. trachea; 3. bronchial
tube; 4. lung; 5. epiglottis; 6. larynx;
7. diaphragm

Page 48
1. lung; 2. lung; 3. contracted
diaphragm; 4. relaxed diaphragm;
5. inhale; 6. exhale

Page 49
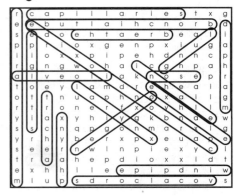

Page 50

Page 51
Results and conclusions will vary.

Page 52
Answers will vary.

Page 53
Charts will vary.

Pages 54–55
1. circulatory system; 2. blood;
3. heart; 4. plasma; 5. red blood
cells; 6. white blood cells; 7. platelets;
8. blood vessels; 9. artery;
10. capillaries; 11. veins 12. valve;
13. atrium; 14. ventricle; 15. vena
cava; 16. oxygen; 17. aorta

Page 56
1. vena cava; 2. valve; 3. right
atrium; 4. valve; 5. right ventricle;
6. aorta; 7. left atrium; 8. pulmonary
artery; 9. pulmonary veins; 10. left
ventricle

Answer Key

Page 57
3, 1, 4, 2

Page 58

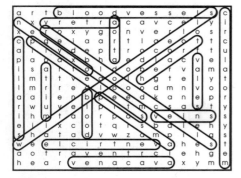

Page 59

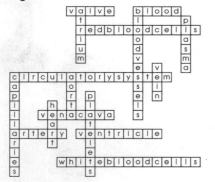

Page 60
Results and conclusions will vary.

Page 61
Travelogues will vary.

Page 62
Answers will vary.

Page 63
Charts will vary.

Page 64
1. excretory system; 2. lungs; 3. skin;
4. kidneys; 5. urine; 6. nephrons;
7. ureter; 8. bladder; 9. urethra

Page 65
1. lung; 2. ureter; 3. urethra; 4. skin;
5. kidney; 6. bladder

Page 66

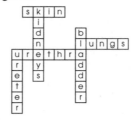

Page 67
Charts will vary.

Page 68
1. endocrine system; 2. gland
3. hormones; 4. pituitary gland;
5. adrenal gland; 6. thyroid gland;
7. parathyroid glands; 8. pancreas;
9. ovaries; 10. testes

Page 69
1. pituitary gland; 2. adrenal glands;
3. pancreas; 4. testes; 5. parathyroid
glands; 6. thyroid gland; 7. ovaries

Page 70
1. ovaries; 2. hormones;
3. pancreas; 4. endocrine;
5. pituitary; 6. parathyroid;
7. adrenal; 8. testes; 9. thyroid

Page 71
Charts will vary.

Pages 72–73
1. nervous system; 2. stimuli;
3. neurons; 4. cell body;
5. dendrites; 6. axon; 7. impulse;
8. synapse; 9. sensory; 10. motor;
11. association; 12. brain; 13. spinal
cord; 14. central; 15. cerebrum;
16. cerebellum; 17. medulla;
18. peripheral; 19. reflex

Page 74
1. medulla; 2. cerebellum; 3. brain
stem; 4. cerebrum; 5. spinal cord

Page 75
1. axon endings; 2. nucleus;
3. cell body; 4. axon; 5. dendrites

Page 76
1. b; 2. a; 3. d; 4. e; 5. c; twenty-five
percent

Page 77

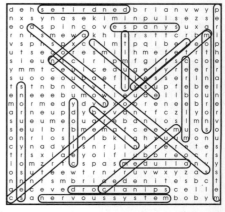

Pages 78–79

Page 80
Answers will vary.

Page 81
Charts will vary.

Page 82
1. skin; 2. epidermis; 3. epithelial;
4. keratin; 5. melanin; 6. dermis;
7. sweat glands; 8. pores; 9. hair
follicles; 10. oil glands

Page 83
1. hair; 2. oil gland; 3. hair follicle;
4. blood vessels; 5. pore;
6. epidermis; 7. nerve cells;
8. dermis; 9. sweat gland; 10. fat
cells

Answer Key

Page 84
Descriptions of results will vary. Conclusions: Temperature receptors in the skin become accustomed to the temperature of the water and do not send new impulses to the brain unless there is a temperature change. Temperature receptors can sense relative changes in temperature. For the hand that was in cold water, the other water seems warm by comparison. Likewise, the hand that was in the warm water senses that the other water is colder.

Page 85
1. cornea; 2. iris; 3. pupil; 4. lens; 5. retina; 6. rods; 7. cones; 8. optic nerve; 9. cerebrum

Page 86
1. cornea; 2. iris; 3. pupil; 4. lens; 5. retina; 6. optic nerve; 7. iris; 8. pupil

Page 87
A. 8; B. 1; C. 6; D. 3; E. 5; F. 7; G. 4; H. 9; I. 2; Magic Number = 15

Page 88

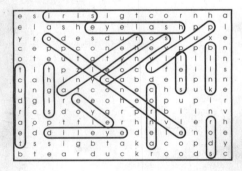

Page 89
Results and conclusions will vary.

Page 90

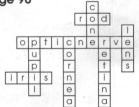

Page 91
1. ear; 2. outer ear; 3. auditory canal; 4. eardrum; 5. earwax; 6. middle ear; 7. bones; 8. cochlea; 9. auditory nerve; 10. semicircular canals

Page 92
1. semicircular canals; 2. anvil; 3. hammer; 4. auditory canal; 5. eardrum; 6. stirrup; 7. eustachian tube; 8. cochlea

Page 93
1. middle ear; 2. hammer; 3. anvil; 4. stirrup; 5. eustachian tube; 6. eardrum; 7. auditory nerve; 8. cochlea; 9. semicircular canals; 10. inner ear; 11. auditory canal; 12. outer ear

Page 94
A. 9; B. 2; C. 7; D. 4; E. 6; F. 8; G. 5; H. 10; I. 3; Magic Number = 18

Page 95

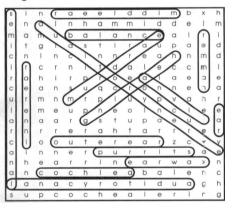

Page 96
1. cartilage; 2. nostrils; 3. nasal passages; 4. mucus; 5. cilia; 6. receptor cells; 7. olfactory nerve; 8. olfactory bulb

Page 97

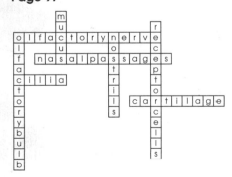

Page 98

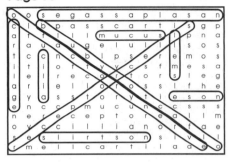

Page 99
Conclusions will vary.

Page 100
1. tongue; 2. taste buds; 3. saliva; 4. taste pores; 5. receptor cells; 6. sweet; 7. salty; 8. sour; 9. bitter; 10. smell

Page 101

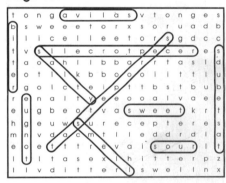

Page 102

Page 103
1. brain; 2. nasal passage; 3. nostril; 4. olfactory nerve; 5. sweet; 6. salty; 7. sour; 8. bitter

Answer Key

Page 104
Results:

bitter
sour
sweet
salty

Conclusions will vary.

Page 105
Paragraphs will vary.

Page 106
1. tongue; sour; 2. ears; loud;
3. nose; smells bad; 4. skin; sharp or painful; 5. eyes; bright; 6. ears; loud;
7. tongue; sour; 8. eyes; dark or hard to see; 9. nose; smells appetizing;
10. skin; sharp or painful;
Descriptions will vary.

Page 107
Drawings will vary.

Page 108
Meals will vary.

Page 109
A. 2; B. 9; C. 4; D. 7; E. 5; F. 3; G. 6;
H. 1; I. 8; Magic Number = 15

Page 110
Answers will vary.

Page 111

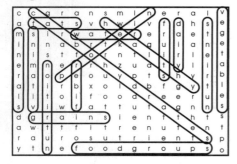

Page 112
Poems will vary.

Page 113
1. Help me.; 2. You are joking.;
3. much better than the rest; 4. I have a problem or complaint about you.; 5. Don't act impolite or rude toward someone who is helping you.; 6. Good luck.; 7. He's clumsy.;
8. Be emotionally attached to a project or cause.; 9. Don't be a smarty-pants.; 10. Acts should be repaid with the same thing that happened to you.; 11. not listening or paying attention; 12. Take a strong position and refuse to budge.; 13. Don't say something stupid.; 14. I'm getting nervous.;
15. inexperienced; 16. being very open and honest—what you see is what you get; 17. Take a chance or risk something.; 18. Hurry up.; 19. A situation has been reversed.; 20. making broad claims or speaking very obnoxiously

Page 114
1. I'm ready to listen.; 2. a favorite or focus of your attention; 3. Stop talking or be quiet.; 4. Loyalty to family is stronger than friendship.;
5. speaking without prior preparation; 6. Something is more than it appears to be.; 7. Make no mistake.; 8. to strongly lead someone; 9. Keep working hard without distractions.; 10. Hope for the best.; 11. feeling very excited or uplifted; 12. Gain some experience or try something new.; 13. being aware of everything going on around you; 14. to be embarrassed;
15. very expensive; 16. Make the best impression you can. 17. to persevere; refuse to give up in the face of adversity;
18. Something is not an inconvenience; it's not a problem.;
19. to take a strong position that is not negotiable; 20. Don't be overwhelmed by a situation.

Page 115
1. toe; 2. elbow; 3. ankle; 4. eyes;
5. nose; 6. hand; 7. eye; 8. ear;
9. skin; 10. leg; 11. rib cage; 12. eye

Page 116
1. liver; 2. pancreas; 3. heart; 4. ribs;
5. skull; 6. cerebellum; 7. pharynx;
8. gallbladder
